A Life Not Wasted

BOB MACDONALD

DEDICATION

This book is for my wife, Judy, who has walked beside me every step of this journey since the first day we met. Without her courage, understanding, prayers and patience, this book would have had a much different ending.

CONTENTS

Acknowledgements 1

Foreword 2

Introduction 6

1 Genesis of an Alcoholic 11

2 Life is not Always Fair 29

3 That Guy 43

4 Basic Training 55

5 Ships and Ports 67

6 Back Home 88

7 Hook, Line and Sinker 102

8 Darkest Before the Dawn 120

9 Sobering Times 134

10 Cross Country 150

11 A Few Tough Years 167

12 The End is in Sight 183

13 Detox 207

14 The 28 Day Program 223

15 Management 239

16 Second Chance 256

About the Cover 270

About the Author 272

ACKNOWLEDGEMENTS

This project started so that my three children, ten grandchildren and one great grandchild would have a way to know me when I am gone. What has become clear through the writing of this book is that without them this journey would have had little meaning.

I would not be who I am without all of the people whom I continue to learn from in the world of recovery, both clients and counsellors, along with all the various groups I am currently involved with.

I need to also mention the countless authors I have absorbed over the years. I have done my level best to adopt your wisdoms into my own life. I am the culmination of all these influences and therefore owe them all a tremendous debt of gratitude.

FOREWORD

Ever heard the word, "Square"?

Well that was me before my journey of learning began. I became involved in a self-help group to help criminals reintegrate and not re-offend (addiction often goes hand in hand with criminality) and now I am the President of this group, the Seventh Step Society of Canada. That's how I met another volunteer, the author of this book, Bob MacDonald; a founding member of our Annapolis Valley Chapter. Thanks to the Seventh Step Society, I began to learn about addiction.

Having been involved in the criminal justice system for almost 30 years, I felt both confident and ignorant about addiction and I'm pretty sure 99% of those I worked with in the system (Crown attorneys, defense lawyers, judges, court staff, probation, parole and corrections workers) had the same ignorance/lack of knowledge.

Instead of learning and understanding addiction, I plodded along with only 5% or so of the needed knowledge. Heck, all of us have a contact, an uncle, a neighbor, maybe a friend that had a substance use problem, and if you're like me, you knew about AA/NA but not what went on there. You have also likely been disappointed when someone you know or love has slipped or fallen off the wagon. We feel that perhaps he/she wasn't trying hard enough and therefore feel that our trust has been broken. We may have even discarded or banished that person from our friendship, love and support.

And, we could always add, for our own comfort, that we just didn't want to "enable" them.

Once in a while, I caught a hint of what I didn't know but needed to appreciate. I was jolted one day, sitting in court, listening to someone being sentenced. Now at this phase of the process, the judge has a remarkable ability to "touch" someone -- the last moment before they leave either through the front door or in the Sheriff's van. The judge in this case said to this particular defendant that "nearly 75% of the criminal cases that come to this court involve alcohol or drug use". A staggering number.

Property offences, driving charges, offences of violence and drug charges often have a connection to addiction. In a disturbing number of cases they either cause these offenses directly or were active when the offense occurred. If you're skeptical, look at government statistics for male and female offenders

I now have a lot of great friends that are recovered/recovering addicts. I'm interested in understanding addiction, and marvel when I have a chance to attend an open meeting, which is usually for a "birthday celebration". I have a book on the history of NA and have heard about very popular, celebrity-based books on the topic. What makes Bob's book particularly attractive to me, "the Square" is how easy it is to read and how honest and frank he is throughout, sharing things most of us would probably not. Bob explains how addiction can happen, how it develops and how it sustains itself. He also explains how friends and family can promote it, how a job can support it and how long it takes to make fundamental changes. There are many memorable quotes, but the most telling for me is: "my first drink was my last social drink."

As a lawyer, I have regularly told the person on the other side of the desk, "I know how you feel". The client appreciates that, but often looks slightly puzzled, perhaps thinking "thanks, but you can't; this is a complicated story". Well, Bob's story has several levels and layers as well but really is easy to understand and I guarantee you'll feel much more informed and have a better toolbox when dealing with someone who may be suffering.

Thank you, Bob for having the courage to share the intimate details of your story.

Mark Knox
National President, 7th Step Society of Canada

INTRODUCTION

This is not just my journey. It is also about two generations of my family going through addiction and recovery. I hope this open, frank, and honest look at our lives will aid you in finding peace in yours. I've been in recovery and in the helping field for most of my adult life, and if I have learned one thing for sure it's that you are responsible for your own life. However, while it is true that your journey is yours, it doesn't mean that you have to travel it alone.

We all ultimately walk our own path, but like all seekers of truth, it is very helpful to find guides who have intimate knowledge of the ground we are about to cover.

What I am able to do is share what I have experienced in my life and what I learned about myself both within addiction and as a result of my own recovery process. I will, throughout the book, share insights from both my father and mother who dealt with their own addiction and recovery journeys. They were so important in helping me as I struggled through this illness. I have learned that this is truly a family disease and that as a result it is families that need treatment.

Has the process been valuable? Well, it has been for me and mine, but any attempt at honest self-reflection, in whatever form, is a helpful exercise. That which has value for one may have value for others; and therefore, it is my sincere hope that you get something out of this as well.

Trust me, I've asked myself what the hell I'm doing writing a book in the first place, and the honest answer is that after walking my path I think I have some insights that can possibly shed some light on this for others. I've started on a few occasions and even had a fair start a few years ago, but always for unknown reasons walked away. I then began writing weekly blogs, (www.justrecoveryconsulting.com) on the topic of recovery for almost two years, looking at addiction through the prism of my own life, and discovered that I actually enjoyed the writing process along the way.

So here we are.

To turn all those blogs into a book was a suggestion from my son. I floated the idea out to a few of my blog readers and received some very positive feedback. Once the decision was made, the next question was what kind of book would it be? I don't lean toward any one genre, as I'm interested in a wide range of topics, and since my own life covers a lot of varied territory, I figured I would just write whatever came out and leave that question for you to answer. They say you should write about what you know. Well, I know my life and what I've experienced better than anyone else, so I figured that's as good a place as any to start.

I will try to be as honest as I can, but since any stories told over many years take on a life of their own I'll have to rely on the memory of those close to me to help shed further light on anything I write about and not rely only on just my memory. Anyone who knows an addict knows we are not known for our accurate recall of events.

Keep in mind, however, that a lot of my time will be spent trying to describe how these events made me feel more so than perhaps the details of all the events themselves. Of course, no good story can be told without some of the nitty gritty details, so I'll try not to let you down there.

More importantly, however, is how I came to view these events.

My journey follows a predictable path in some respects but not so much in others, which I hope will make this an interesting read for anyone who doesn't know me. I will not, to my knowledge, put any individual other than myself in an uncomfortable position in the writing of this so everyone who knows me can take a nice deep breath; nor will I reveal something that may put me in a place that could cause me harm now. I'm pretty sure if stupidity was a chargeable offence, I'd be behind bars already, so those are all the things you will hear about in this book, even though at the time my decisions seemed to me to be absolutely brilliant.

This is not a "poor me" or a "tell-all" book but more of a "share-all" kind of thing because I do believe I would not be who I am today if I had not experienced every single event along the way. If anyone gets something out of it as a result of me sharing, all the better.

Let me just take this quick moment to say "thanks, Life" -- for all the hard and soft lessons along the way, and for not making me repeat too many of them. If I know anything, it is that lessons will be repeated until learned, and that most lessons are learned in the trenches. Life, however, is too sweet to be spent in the trenches all the time and should be enjoyed whenever and wherever possible.

I suppose I also started this project with the idea that it would give my grandkids an insight into who "Grampie" or "Papa" was, and to pass along what I learned in the hopes they might avoid some of my mistakes. I hope they might gain in some way from the events of my journey, and now that I've decided to publish it, that same hope extends to you. If it helps one person, the many attempts and the hours put in will have been more than worth all the effort. If you're currently struggling, please know that I've been there, and this is how I came out of it.

Every story, task or journey has a beginning. So, let's start there.

1 THE GENESIS OF AN ALCOHOLIC

In the beginning... oh, wait that line has been taken.

Well, there is a beginning to everything, and that includes me. I was born the fourth son of our family in December 1948 shortly after my father sobered up. That means I've been on the planet for seventy-odd years and have been, in some way, under the influence of alcohol for all of them. I haven't been using alcohol all of that time, obviously, but it has been part of my life from the beginning.

Side Note: See, this is why I enjoy this process so much! That insight just came to me as

I started writing this today.

I was born about two years or so after my two-year-old brother Donny perished in a house fire that my father caused after passing out with a lit cigarette (as far as they could determine). Booze took my brother away before I was even born. I guess in retrospect alcohol was a major influence on me before I was even conceived.

Whether I was drinking it or not alcohol has played a huge part in who I have become but if you add up the actual time I drank, it totals only ten years. As with other alcoholics, not all my drinking days were horrendous, and to be honest -- a fair amount of it was really just plain fun.

Until it wasn't.

After my brother Donnie died, my mother and two older brothers stayed at the home of a family friend for some time. Although Aunt Bette and Uncle Max weren't even really related to us, they stepped up and were there as my father began his own journey of sobering up. It never fails to amaze me that when a person is ready to change, people appear to help them.

Shortly after that, the family got back on its feet and we moved to a small village in Nova Scotia called Kinsac, a rural community about 35 km north of Halifax. I was born at some point during that transition after the fire though I obviously have no memory of the event. My paternal grandfather had a cottage there in the village that we moved into until the DVA (Department of Veterans Affairs) helped dad with a loan to buy a small farm of eleven acres just up the road. This was home until I joined the navy eighteen years later and played an important role in forming who I would become as an adult.

I'd say the first five years of my life went by and I hardly remember much if any of it. I do have some memories from that time but whether they are actual memories or stories I've merely adopted as memories is very hard to determine. Some of these early memories are vague recollections while others are remarkably clear. I remember waking up in the cold and never wanting to get out of bed, playing with cars under the front porch in the yard, and being afraid of going down into the dirt basement.

I remember playing in the pile of laundry on Saturdays and liking the smell – somewhat weird now that I write it – but I was a child whose world was still very small. Some of the clearer, early, memories I have were of meeting dad at the train station and being carried home on his shoulders. I'd be very young for those ones.

I can still picture the beautiful frost artwork on the windows on those cold mornings. My imagination would always make them into magical forests. I remember sitting with my grandfather as he told me stories of when he was a young boy growing up on their farm in Halifax and, of course, his quintessentially Canadian hockey stories of his exploits as a player in the 20's, 30's and even 40's.

I remember laying out in hayfields, looking at the sky and smelling that clean loamy air. We would make tunnels as kids in the high hay and try to sneak up on each other. In the evenings the hay field was full of fireflies which we would catch in glass bottles. The barn and chicken house were where I spent a lot of time. The chickens always scared me when mom and I would go and collect eggs. Some of them didn't like you taking their eggs and would give you a peck if they could get a clean shot in. I got even with them when I got a little older and a little cleverer. I would put a noose under the straw and catch them by the legs when they stepped inside it.

This was great fun until dad figured out why the chickens had stopped laying eggs. It was a foolish thing to do but I didn't know any better at the time. I remember feeling very sorry for them when dad had to slaughter some for the table. I also remember the sight of a headless chicken running around, but it's probably not surprising that memory would stay with me.

The barn! I spent so many hours in that barn, both alone and with my friends. We had so many good times in there, it could probably fill another whole book, for sure. I had the run of the place even as a very little guy. We would jump from the cross beams into the haymow until the hay got too low and we would hit the hidden floor with a jolt that would end that fun until the next year. We would play tag in the barn, and to avoid getting tagged would run across the cross beams high above the main floor.

My mother would tell the story of me at about four years old, going out to the barn after she had dressed me in a white outfit to go to town with a warning to stay clean. We had a bull calf called Ferdinand who I decided to try to ride with less than stellar results. Wet bull shit and white outfits do not go well together, as my mother discovered. Not long after this incident Ferdinand got out of his pen and ate some loose insulation and died. He was buried with full honours on the hill in our upper pasture.

To answer the unasked question, yes, the pigs were still green when slaughtered. If we wanted to go to Halifax, we would take the train. Back then it was an honest to God steam engine. The conductors loved to see me get on the train as they liked to tease me and then stand by and have a good laugh as I cursed them out (much to my mother's dismay). My patience, even back then, was lacking. Mom told me about one time after I watched several buses pass us by that when ours finally stopped to pick us up, I cursed out the driver for passing us by so many times. I had no idea that those other buses that drove by were not the right ones.

Precocious little bugger, wasn't I?

When I was about six or seven, my friend Allan and I decided to try riding the pigs. They chased us out of the pen and in an act of youthful retaliation we took a paint brush that was handy and applied a liberal amount of green paint to the offenders. While we were in a working mood, Allan and I also painted over the windows as well. I got in a lot of trouble for that one.

For some reason dad never did clean the windows and they stayed that way until he sold the property many years later.

Watching pigs get slaughtered is a vivid memory which has stayed with me. I recall one of our neighbours coming over with a pistol and trying to shoot them, but his gun didn't even knock them out since they have extremely thick skulls. We had to resort to the old method of a maul, and while stunned we cut their throats; definitely not for the squeamish. Dunking the pigs in a huge vat of boiling water in order to help the process of scraping the hair off them was for some strange reason fascinating to me. I remember dad giving me the ears, but I can't remember the reason why he did so. I was a bit of a strange little guy. And no, that's not going to be the end of the barn stories.

Despite the picture I've painted of my early youth, we actually were supervised, though from what I've written thus far, it probably doesn't sound like it. I know I put my mother through her own kind of hell trying to keep tabs on what we were up to once we had full mobility and free rein.

What I know now is that all the mothers in the village were watching over us. If mom was looking for me, she would shout my name, and it would pass down the road from mother to mother, and I would eventually hear it and come home. My friend Rob Larder's mother was the odd one out and she would blow a whistle that was so loud we swore it could be heard in Toronto.

All the mothers went to the lake with us and kept a careful eye on us until we could each swim across the lake and back with no problem. Our dog Judy a Water Spaniel was always with us, but never swam and absolutely hated the water, despite her breeding. After swimming the lake, we were set free and had the run of the village and lake. The beach where I learned to swim at four years old became too tame for us eventually, and we all swam at the diving rocks. More than one of us scraped our chest trying to clear submerged rocks when the water was low, but no serious injuries occurred -- we knew where every rock was and trusted our own abilities.

The lake became the center of our young lives in both summer and winter. Staying inside was something foreign to us, and for me only a good book might delay me getting outdoors.

Once we were deemed old enough, the shackles came off and the entire countryside became our playground. That is a freedom that may not be possible any more in our society. It doesn't seem like it anyway. If it's true, I think we're all much worse off as a result.

We would get up in the morning, run outside, and make our own fun. And we did. God, how we did. We were creative, innovative, and adventurous and came up with all kinds of ways to have a good time. Some of these activities were on the dangerous side but provided hours if not days of just plain fun. You see kids playing road hockey on the pavement now, but back then we played it on the gravel road and when facing a shot, the ball was often accompanied by pieces of gravel. I feel we were a tougher breed back then because we were not coddled.

Oh, by the way, I smoked grass when I was about ten.

Well, I guess it was actually dry hay, which was hollow, and if you lit it you could draw in smoke. I can tell you it burned and was so strong that I coughed for hours. I did try smoking tobacco a bit later on, with one of my friends who had stolen a couple of cigarettes from his father and I think we ate a half a row of carrots to get the taste out of our mouths.

I did, however, take my first drink at around the same time. If my memory serves me, I recall my partner in crime and I stole some beer out of somebody's trunk and went to a little barn below his place and drank it. I can't remember if I got sick or not, but I know I certainly got a buzz on.

I don't think of this as addiction in any way, just youthful experimentation and deviltry. Most youngsters are curious by nature and unfortunately some lose it as they grow up. The fifties and sixties were a time for the curious at heart because so many wondrous things were beginning to be introduced into our community.

Our phone was attached to the wall, not our hip. It was a party line, which meant that anyone on the line could pick up and listen to whatever conversation was going on (and they often did). Our phone number was one long and two short rings, and it rang on all the phones along the line, so people knew you were the one being called.

If you wanted to use the phone, you picked up the receiver and if someone was already "on the line" talking, you would have to wait until they were done. You would know when people were finished because they would crank a very short ring. If it was very important, you'd just say so and the other people would hang up. Can you imagine that being the case today?

I remember running home from school to watch the World Series games, back when they played a lot of afternoon weekday games. All of this was shown in glorious, snowy, black and white.

I forget how many people were on our party line, but it was most of the forty to fifty families in our village I would think. It was frustrating if you were talking to someone and people kept picking up to make a call. If they stayed on to listen in, the signal would get weak. The more people who listened the weaker it would get until you would have to tell them all to get off so you could hear who you were speaking to.

One of the big events of my youth was when we

got our first television. We were fortunate enough to have one of the first ones in the whole village, so our living room was always packed with kids on Saturday mornings for either cartoons or wrestling. After we watched wrestling, we would then immediately go outside and try all the different moves we had seen on each other. The only difference was that for us there was no padded ring or training.

We would get the Saturday night hockey games at the start of the second period and three generations of MacDonalds would sit and watch together. Each one of us would have a different take on the game and it could get pretty heated. There were often a few friends in this mix as well and everyone was either a fan of the Montreal Canadians or the Toronto Maple Leafs. I was the odd man out because I was a Boston Bruins fan, like my gramps and dad.

When I was really little, I used to sneak down the stairway and sit on the second step of the stairs because from that little perch I could see the TV. Mom and dad couldn't see me but after a while I guess they would sense my presence because they would always yell at me to go to bed. The two TV stations we got (I think there were just two) would sign off at midnight and only broadcast the "test pattern" until it came back on sometime in mid-morning.

But it was never about the TV for me back then during the summer.

We would spend days building camps in the woods

with knives and hatchets and then use them as a base to go exploring all the land around us. The winter was the time for TV as the days were so short.

I can still picture a large stand of pines behind our land that felt other-worldly. Now that I think about it, it was most likely an old-growth stand that has since been cut down in the building of the golf course. But it doesn't matter, because it still lives on in my mind. As does the river, and fishing holes we spent forever playing in and around, which have also become part of that golf course. The course is called "Lost Creek" but that area was not lost to those of us who grew up there.

When I think of a quiet place of peace, the bluff at the foot of the falls is what comes to mind. Even after all this time it is still very clear in my mind's eye. The amount of times I fell in that river and survived is crazy, but I always went back. We'd be out fishing in April, trying to get across or find a good spot, and fall into the spring flood water. Do you have any idea how cold that is? We would also jump from ice chunk to ice chunk during the spring break-up and often fall in. Fortunately, our friends were always there to haul us out.

In the winter, the best ice was always near where the river entered the lake, but it was also the thinnest. We took so many chances playing hockey in that area, chasing stray pucks onto ice that would break under your feet if you didn't skate fast enough. If we fell in there the current would have taken us under the ice and the body would most likely not be found till spring.

How the hell any of us survived those early years is beyond me. I suppose it was a precursor of things to come.

The woods surrounding the village was another haven for our exploring minds. We always carried knives and often hatchets in the woods with us and usually a trusty slingshot as well. It wasn't until later that we took bows and firearms, all of which we became very proficient with. I once took a piece of groove and tongue lumber and made a very functional crossbow, complete with a trigger mechanism. Throwing knives and hatchets was a pastime we all participated in, and we would compete against each other all the time. These are just some of the skills we got really good at.

My cousin almost lost his eye one day when the boys were practicing throwing spears. He stepped out from behind the target just as someone threw one. I know this sounds like a story from ancient Sparta, but it was really just Kinsac, Nova Scotia, in the fifties and sixties.

We would play a particular kind of tag above the ground in a tightly packed group of spruce trees. I think this proved that we were indeed the first generation out of the trees. If we found a tree in the woods that had fallen over but got hung up, we would climb it, and jump up and down until it let go. We would then ride it to the ground. This activity could have gone wrong in so many ways, and I shudder to think about it now.

We knew every path in the woods for miles around and would take shortcuts to get where we wanted to go, saving time and distance. My favourite area was up the Falls Road to Beaver Bank Lake. There were so many great places along the road like the railway bridge, the falls, sucker hole and the gage house which had a pulley car across the river.

The pulley car was dangerous, and we mostly left it alone after one of the guys nearly lost his finger after it was caught between the pulley and the cable. But we did catch some nice trout there, and all along the river, so we never stopped going.

We were careful when crossing the bridge but on one occasion one of the guys got caught by a train and had to jump off the bridge. He was lucky enough to land on one of the supports, but that was close to being it for him.

We had more than a few close calls around the trains. I was once playing tag on the box cars – not a very safe proposition, when I fell from the top, missed the first rung of the ladder and landed on a pile of connector plates. I busted up my arm pretty good, which was sore for week or so, but I couldn't tell mom where I injured it because we weren't supposed to be playing around the trains in the first place. Risky behaviour and keeping secrets were already becoming locked in as a part of my MO.

The tracks were just a part of our playground, and you had to cross them to get to the lake where we went swimming, fishing, and skating. We would put pennies on the rail and trains would flatten them down to paper thin disks which we thought was pretty cool. We were warned that this could cause a derailment but didn't believe a tiny penny could ever manage to damage a huge train and so tried a few nails to test our theory. I'm proud to say we never lost one train.

We used the gypsum that fell from the open cars as chalk to draw on rocks or any other surface it would stay on. All along the tracks grew blueberries but the best place was about two miles up past the head of the lake which was also where we picked cranberries in the fall.

Our back field was the defacto community ball field, and we all kept it mowed and straightened out. We even built our own backstop. We were pretty adept at making whatever we needed because there was no money for non-essential things. Our ball field had a short left field where it went uphill and was covered with scrub, and after we got older it was a ground rule out if you hit it there because it was so hard to find the ball.

After dad banned me from shooting pucks at the garage doors and inside the barn, I turned to the backstop and slowly beat that to pieces as well. The barn had a pitched roof and it was angled in such a way that when you threw a ball at it, it would return a high fly ball. I would practice throwing and catching for hours. I would spend hours on my own practicing these activities. I guess I enjoyed the solitude and was always quite comfortable keeping my own company.

We set up obstacle courses in the barn with a climbing rope and punching bag and we would work out, run on the beams, and jump into the hay like the untamed wild things we were.

There was a game we called "Annie Over", and to this day I don't know where the name came from. The Munro's mother's name was Annie, so that is a possibility. Two teams were on each side of the barn and one team threw a ball over to the other; then the team with the ball would run around and try to hit someone on the other team to eliminate the opponent. You had to guess which way the others would run to be in position to hit someone. Those games could last a long time, and did we ever get in good shape!

We used to play hockey against Fall River which was at the end of the lake (about three miles away). We would skate down and play all day and then skate home after we were done. One way or the other, that skate home always seemed to be right into the wind!

Skating against the wind had us following the shoreline to stay out of it as much as possible, which increased the distance considerably. I started playing goalie because we made nets with two-by-fours and chicken wire and after we were finished, we realized that we'd now need real goalies.

My gear was cobbled together from baseball stuff I had, and an old set of goalie pads. The gear was not very good. Bruises were standard after every game. I practiced by having the guys shoot pucks at me in front of the garage door until we wrecked the door completely, but as a result I got pretty good (or so I thought).

All ages played together in those days, from early teens to adults, and there was no quarter given. Two of the hardest hits I ever received were on that lake by guys much older than me. It hurt, but it sure taught me to keep my head up. A lesson in life I suppose, not just in hockey.

We never played any organized sports until we were well into our teen years. The first thing I got into was junior baseball where the Beaver Bank and Kinsac kids played against other surrounding communities in Halifax County. It really was a pretty good competitive league and we had lots of family and friends who would come out and watch us.

I was a pretty decent catcher who had a really good arm and enjoyed being in on every play, as catchers are. They tried me out as pitcher once, and I was doing well but when I threw one over the backstop our coach yanked me, and that was the end of my pitching career. I wasn't a bad infielder, and decent outfielder as well, but I loved catching because of the involvement in the game.

Becoming a goalie seemed like a natural extension when the opportunity presented itself. They refer to catchers' equipment as the "tools of ignorance" -- I guess because of the probability of injury and the physical nature of the position. I guess looking back I was always trying to prove to myself that I was good enough and took on the hardest positions.

In high school I played some hockey but only ended up playing one year. I had been a goalie to that point and then just decided to play defence instead. I had little experience playing out, so I didn't turn any heads in the tryouts. We had a quasi-junior team we put together ourselves and played in Lantz, NS against some other local teams. That's where I discovered the physical part of the game, something that became what I was known for later in my hockey career.

I think I was fifteen or sixteen years old before I played in an indoor rink. That's when I switched from goalie to defence because the gear I used was horrible and the shots were getting much harder; the bruises and soreness were escalating. I put on much lighter gear and blocked shots instead. Look, nobody ever accused me of being smart!

I don't know what to say about my love of sport. I just loved competing and testing myself against other people, and myself, and I suppose that has stayed with me to this day. It's a good way of staying sharp in many ways. Looking back now I can see that it allowed me to be in the moment with nothing on my mind except what was right in front of me.

Those days were incredible in so many ways and provided me a sound foundation which I would later desperately need. I would lose some of that feeling of curiosity and joy for life for a number of years due to events which had a deep impact on my outlook, and I only reclaimed my zest for life when I was in recovery.

2 LIFE IS NOT ALWAYS FAIR

All of us kids took part in any activity that was going on in our community but, as I mentioned before, sometimes I would bow out to go read. I think it's because I read a lot that I had a fairly extensive vocabulary and pretty soon I started to be mocked when I spoke any word not common to my peer group. Physically I was a tough kid, but I was also a very sensitive kid and I took the mockery to heart.

Not too long ago I went to a family gathering out in Kinsac and one of the guys I grew up with asked me if I was still reading "all them books". I just smiled and said that I was. Funny how even nearly 60 years later I was still remembered for reading "all them books". I wish they could have experienced all the places and adventures I enjoyed while sitting in my room those many rainy afternoons, then perhaps they too might have discovered the joy of getting lost in a book. Reading has opened so many doors to knowledge that I never would have been exposed to if I wasn't a reader.

I think this disconnect with my friends was where I started to feel like I was different and didn't belong. I kept reading, however, that never stopped but I did keep my vocabulary in line with everyone else. Years later, I now see this as a turning point where I started trying to change who I was in order to fit in with other people. That, or I would just avoid interactions where I thought it may be uncomfortable altogether.

Both my parents were big readers as well. This is where I probably picked up my love for books. We had a bus converted into a library (the Bookmobile) which came to the village once a month and everyone would walk down to where it parked to return books and pick up the next month's reading. This was, for me, something I looked forward to and couldn't wait to discover my next new adventure.

I think, as a result, storytelling has always been a big part of our family, as well as a way to spend time together. I learned so much about how my grandfather and father grew up from those times. I can remember curling up next to my father to watch TV and would follow him around like a puppy when he worked on the farm and he would tell me stories. Following him around as he was plowing the field was also a great way to fill our worm buckets for fishing.

I was very close to him when I was a little tyke but as soon as I got to be around ten or twelve that all changed. He was away so much for work, and when he got home he was usually very tired. I think it was a combination of my becoming more independent as I got older, and him being gone so much, that made me begin to feel our closeness lessening.

I missed it a lot.

Once I was in my teens, I went my own way and didn't re-establish that closeness again until the last years of his life.

I was in my 50's before I decided consciously to change my own behaviour toward my father in order to reclaim that closeness. I had worked a lot on my personal growth by that time, and at one point I decided that the next time I saw him I would give him a hug and tell him I loved him.

I remember it well. We went for a visit at my brother Pete's house and when I walked in and saw him, I went right over and, instead of shaking hands, gave him a hug and told him I loved him. It was like hugging a tree. There was no response. But despite what I felt was some discomfort on his part I kept doing it, and after a while he did loosen up and start to respond. I think of all the years wasted where our relationship could have been so much closer, but this awareness can only be gained from life experience.

Today I hug my son and tell him I love him, and I have done so since he was young -- thanks to my wife

Judy who kept working on and with me. These cycles can be broken, and you don't have to accept the status quo just because of prior patterns. It was a lesson that took something like forty years to figure out but as I've said before, while I'm not the quickest to catch on, I do eventually get there.

When I was an adolescent, my father taught square dancing and Scottish country dancing. I had to go. This activity also didn't fit in well with the Kinsac mindset at that time. I do recall secretly enjoying it until I was into my teens, but then started losing interest as it wasn't fitting in with the "cool guy" image I was going for. A friend and I gave dad such a hard time about it he finally let us quit. As much as I was annoyed by having to go all those years, I will admit now that it did turn me into a pretty good dancer.

Dad was very active in AA in those early years and would often get a phone call that someone needed help. At those times he would get up and go. He would think nothing of driving long distances and I know he once went to Pictou in order to help a lady who ended up being the first female member of AA in the province. In those days that drive alone took most of the day. We were also used to having dad bring guys home to stay with us until they got their feet under them. You never knew who you would find on the couch in the morning.

I remember we had one guy stay with us for about six months by the name of Red who was an old fighter. That lasted until he took my brother Ted with him to Halifax one day. When they didn't come home, dad had to track them down and finally found them at the bootleggers where Ted was having a bite to eat and Red was hammered. I think mom put her foot down then and wouldn't let dad use our home as a halfway house after that. This was very uncommon behaviour for our community, but dad was doing what he felt he had to do to both stay sober and help others do the same. I think the village thought we were a little strange for doing this.

Another event that put me in a position where I felt different from my friends happened around this time. It was a very impactful period in my life for sure. Let me start by saying that I won't get into any of the nitty, gritty details as I don't want to dignify the actual events with a lot of space here – to do so would give it a power it no longer deserves. But it does need to be addressed, since it was a pivotal event in not just my life, but with regard to my early development.

When I was a young adolescent there was an older person who introduced me to sex way before I was ready. It's something you hear about more and more these days as we're creating an environment where people feel more comfortable about sharing these types of personal experiences. For me, at the time, the encounter was confusing, and would be something that affected my self-esteem much more powerfully than I would know for years to come.

I struggled with writing about this because my intention isn't to bring a focus onto the person in question but, rather, to illustrate how this experience affected me and how I was able to come to terms with it later in life. Who it was is far less important than the fact I am now able to talk about it and have recognized the affect it had on me.

It was traumatic because, like all abuse, it is an abuse of power and made me feel powerless. I was often sick at that time to avoid having to deal with this person and I thank God it didn't last very long. Most of us get curious about sex and experiment with it in many ways when we're young, but to be coerced and manipulated into it before you even know what's happening is far from healthy.

I was lucky in a lot of ways, considering what I now know others have had to deal with in that department, but you can only judge your life from your own experience and for me, at that time, it was a very difficult thing to deal with. Like so many others I tried to ignore it and stuffed it way down deep. But such things don't remain dormant forever, and at some point, I would have to come to terms with it in order to heal.

Many years later that young boy that I was and a much older version of himself had a very frank conversation with each other and decided that since he was not responsible for what happened it was time to let it go. We agreed that the person who did those things had an illness, and we agreed to accept that though it had happened, we would no longer let the experience affect the rest of our lives. It had done so, of course, to a great degree right up until "we" reached that understanding. Had it not been for the process of recovery from my own illness of addiction, that breakthrough may not have been possible.

The only reason I bring this forward is because it was, and is, part of my life experience and to hide it is not being honest. I feel very strongly that this is the very nature of what I'm trying to do with this book and so it's something I felt compelled to spend some time on.

After working for years with people struggling with addiction as well as those who have been incarcerated, it has become clear that abuse -- whether sexual, physical or emotional -- plays a major role in these later conditions. My wife, who worked in mental health for many years, has said that it is also very prevalent in people who seek help with mental health issues as well.

I won't say it is the cause of these conditions later in life, but I do feel comfortable saying that the evidence is overwhelming that it plays a heavy role in many of these troubles manifesting later on.

The strange thing is that I can now actually say that I am also able to see the positives of going through this as a youngster, (yes, even those become possible when you gain deeper perspective) and I see now that having gone through that difficult experience and come out the other side, I have a much better ability to connect with others who have been through similar circumstances. This is especially helpful when you're trying to counsel someone and get through to them when they are hurting. Shared personal experience can break down many walls and it's always been my hope that by sharing my own story with others I may be helping them acknowledge and possibly overcome their own abuse issues in even a small way.

I know it can be an uncomfortable topic because the subject is so painful. It can also be a formidable "trigger", and for many can hit a little too close to home. But it's precisely because it does touch so many people that I feel it is so important to share. I know the people who grew up with me will start trying to figure who it was. Don't bother. The person is no longer living, and it was no one I was really close to at that time.

Let's just say, if you are reading this, it definitely wasn't you.

The other major event I remember being very traumatic as a youngster, perhaps even more so than the previous experience, was a beating I took at about age ten from my grandfather. It happened in our kitchen at mealtime, and it turned my world upside down.

Before I get into that event, let me paint a picture for you. My Grandfather (Gramps) had a massive stroke in his early to mid-fifties. His doctor at the time told dad to take him out to the farm in Kinsac as he only had a few months to live and the country would be a nice place for him.

Gramps was a tough customer though and ended up outliving the doctor by several years. He passed away when he was seventy-seven and during that time suffered several more strokes. He managed to get around with a cane even though his right side was pretty much useless.

I spent hours and hours with him in my younger years and he told me many stories about his youth. He spoke at length about his days as a celebrated hockey player and then later when he worked for the Oland family as an interior decorator. For those who remember the old Capitol Theatre on Barrington Street in Halifax, and how beautiful the interior was, it was largely done by Gramps. I loved listening to those stories and have no doubt they helped form a lot of the interests I would have later in life.

I still have a folding ruler of his and had a jackknife until my grandson unknowingly destroyed it in one of his many ambitious experiments. I did have a set of metal combs which he would use to grain surfaces so that they would take on the appearance of various types of wood, another lost art, but unfortunately, I never learned to use them, and they have disappeared over the years. I also have copies of articles describing his exploits as a hockey player from newspapers during the 1920's. Now that is a cool thing to have, and there is even an article about my dad when he played high school hockey that called him "a chip off the old block."

My grandfather was there until just before I joined the navy and was more of a father figure than my dad was throughout that time. My father traveled more and more as his responsibilities increased as the years went on. Gramps was a constant in our home and when I was younger, he paid a lot of attention to me which made what happened later come as such a shock. It just did not fit into what I knew of the man I worshipped and had lived with for years.

We were sitting at the table one morning and my mother said something to me. I couldn't even tell you what she said or what I said back to her, but I guess it was with a bit of attitude. The next thing I knew I was on the floor.

My grandfather began wailing away on me and all I could do was curl up in a ball and take it. I could hear mom screaming at him to stop but it took a few moments before he did. It must have finally registered what he was doing because without a word he turned away and went to his room.

Mom took me out of the house and down the road. I was sobbing because I was hurt for sure but more so because I was emotionally devastated. I looked up to my grandfather and had spent countless hours with him listening to his stories and learning from him. He was the reason I became interested in drawing, and playing hockey, and many of the things I still have interest in today. I couldn't understand why he had done that to me.

I think the hardest thing about this incident at the time was pretending that nothing out of the ordinary had happened and that everything was normal. I'm sure that mom had a frank conversation with dad regarding the incident since nothing like it ever happened again. My relationship with him was utterly changed from that point forward, and I was always cautious around him; we were no longer close.

I have a number of insights about this particular event that I'll get to later in the book. Suffice it to say that the effects of these various events culminated in a young man who felt like he just didn't fit in, was hesitant to trust people, and learned to keep things to himself. This young man carried these feelings outside of his little community and into an ever-expanding world. Little did I know how many times I would hear similar versions of these events played out in so many other lives struggling with addiction.

High school was where I found that although I was an athlete and, on many teams, I always felt like I really didn't belong. I was good at keeping things to myself by now and had learned to pretend to fit in when dealing with the various circles I moved through. When you think of yourself as not belonging, your self-worth is directly impacted, and this plays out in your (in)ability to feel connected to anyone or anything.

I decided to play senior baseball in high school with the local Bedford team instead of with my Beaver Bank peers, and also began taking a lot of flak for that. By this time, I was spending most of my time in Bedford, but the guys I grew up with saw me as a "traitor" and I was treated accordingly. I no longer felt a part of the Kinsac crowd, and it hurt to feel like I no longer fit in at home. Looking back, this was probably an attempt at a geographical solution to my problems, but I never saw it that way at the time.

I remember one day being told some guy I didn't even know wanted to fight me. It was set up to happen at the Kinsac train station. I went down and all the neighbourhood kids had gathered to see it happen. When the guy I was supposed to fight showed up, I didn't know him from Adam. We were both pretty much the same size so we would have likely done some major damage to each other.

Like I said, I was a fairly tough kid physically and could take a punch as well as the next guy, but I also wasn't stupid. I asked the guy what we were fighting about, and he said he didn't really know, which was strange since he showed up with heavy work boots and rings covering both hands. He was clearly quite geared to go but I wasn't. I saw no good reason to bleed for everyone else's amusement, so I decided not to fight. Like I said, I wasn't stupid.

I know this really disappointed all the local boys and I've often wondered if this was a way to get back at me for playing ball for Bedford. I'll probably never know for certain, but it left a bad taste in my mouth because it sure felt like a setup to me. It cemented the fact that I had outgrown Kinsac (at least in my mind) and was ready to move on.

My academics were taking a downturn at this time, not because I wasn't smart enough but because all I was interested in was sports, girls, and partying. I chose to spend my time on those pursuits and had little interest in schoolwork at all. Once I started failing, it further re-enforced the belief that I was just not good enough and my downward spiral continued. I had learned to pretend I didn't really care, but I did, and my self-worth tanked as a result.

It was around this time that I started drinking.

I was sixteen or so when I started, and I remember very clearly finally feeling connected -- like I was part of something -- for the very first time. I didn't have to try to fit in when I was drinking and was just accepted as a part of the group. It just felt right. For the first time, I had people around me who felt and acted just like me, and that was a great comfort. I had no idea that they were just as lost as I was because when we all drank, we felt we were able to connect to one another.

I was living at home at that point but, in my head, I was pretty much on my own. I still relied on my folks for a car to get around, and so many other things, but I felt like I was on my own. Perhaps I should have just left home right then while I still knew it all.

Our memories become locked in and more solidified with time and form how we see ourselves. I accepted the truth of my interpretation of these events for so long that it was only after many years, and a lot of help, that I began to see them more clearly and address them in a much healthier way. How I felt about them has changed through the years and I'm now much better at placing them in the "lessons learned" category of my mind, rather than in the category of "currently suffering". I understand that to some these events may seem minor and that some might not have even been meant in a hurtful way, but again, the most important part of an event is how we feel about it and how it influences us as a result. Perception, after all, is truth.

I have come to learn that I am a very sensitive person by nature, as most addicted people are, and for us sensitive types the effects of these kinds of events may strike deeper than with others. In fact, I think this is the primary reason we medicate: to dull our emotional pain. But the fact of the matter is, when I started drinking all I did was accumulate more and more weight to this growing burden of emotional baggage.

3 THAT GUY

The first drink I ever had was both my first, and my last social drink. Right out of the gate I got drunk and either passed out or blacked out, I really can't say for sure. All I know is that I really liked the ability to not feel, a lot.

From that day on I drank with a purpose: to get drunk and to become "not me". That insight only was possible to make many years later and was certainly not something I was aware of at the time. I found something in alcohol that could transform this shy, uneasy, guy in social situations into THAT GUY. You know, the one who can talk to the ladies and dance up a storm while exuding pure confidence. It was on! I absolutely loved that feeling.

I wanted to be that guy all the time and the only way I could access him was by getting drunk. To say it was a strong draw would not even begin to explain how powerful the desire was. But the real problem is that I can honestly say that it worked, because as a result of this early behaviour I became popular in that circle of people and, more importantly, was accepted.

I was still an athlete, and when I was actually playing sports, I felt fine. Once the game was over, I slipped back into feeling awkward inside once more and began craving that feeling of acceptance. It wasn't until much later that I found out that "fine" is just an acronym for Fucked up, Insecure, Neurotic and Egotistical (or Emotional).

One of the people I had respect for in school was our physical education teacher, Mr. MacVicar, who always treated me well. He tried to support me when my marks started going bad, and even spoke to my parents for me. Later, in my military career, he wrote a letter of support when I tried to re-muster to the Physical Education and Recreation trade.

I remember one of the older guys I was beginning to hang out with crashed our school dance one time. This guy was trouble for sure, and when Mr. MacVicar put a hand on his shoulder and asked him to leave, the guy sucker punched him and split his lip badly. Mr. MacVicar and I were out on the field a few days later, and he picked up a softball bat and jokingly said, "I think I should have had this with me at the dance."

He never bad-mouthed the guy who punched him, and he could have laid charges but didn't. I really looked up to him even more after that, and stopped hanging around with that particular guy, a decision that probably saved me from what would have followed, as I think he ended up in conflict with the law latter on.

After I had a few drinks in me and was with others who were drinking, I felt comfortable. The problem was that due to my age there just weren't a lot of high school kids who operated like that, so I ended up gravitating to a group of older guys who were no longer in school. Some of these guys were already in trouble with the law and it really is only by sheer luck that I avoided the same fate. I do remember drinking a few times with one of my teachers who I can only assume was trying hard to hold on to his youth, but he was an otherwise great guy.

When I started playing senior baseball for Bedford, I was around sixteen or seventeen, and a lot of the guys I was playing with were family men with jobs. I would drink with those guys and that made me feel really cool. The ball players just accepted me as part of the team and treated me as one of them.

The other guys I was running with were older as well and I think they liked having young guys look up to them; it probably puffed up their ego and made them feel like big shots. When your self-esteem is low and someone favours you and shows you attention, you tend to follow along with them. So, from that point on I became a follower. I could have ended up more than once in trouble with the law like them, but for whatever reason didn't go down that road. I was carrying on the learned behaviour of adjusting myself to fit in with others and as a result began seeking approval from the older guys.

This, I now see, was when school became a "drag" and my attitude continued going south. I failed grade ten and squeaked through my second try at it only by the skin of my teeth. The first year in grade eleven I got suspended -- and I really can't even remember why -- my bad attitude and poor attendance was most likely the cause.

One night a buddy of mine and I decided to break into the school and spend the night, so we left a window open in our classroom earlier that day. We came back after the janitors had left and got in through the window we had left open. We didn't damage anything and only ate some food in the home economics kitchen when we got hungry. We spent most of our time in the gym shooting hoops and left before anyone came in the next morning.

Looking back, it was totally a stupid thing to do and we could have really gotten into trouble but didn't. But this illustrates where my mind was at the time: I was pretty much done with school by this point.

I was working in Bedford at a grocery store on weekends and some evenings and making some money which all went to booze and girls. The store also supplied me with free smokes: I would grab them on my way out because at that time they were displayed at the check-outs and easy to boost. I think the statute of limitations has gone by on that petty thievery, so I'm hoping my admission here counts an amends made, I guess.

I was seldom home and stayed at Aunt Bette's and Uncle Max's in Bedford because that was where the action was. I stayed with them for a couple of years, mostly on weekends and during summers, and they treated me like a son. I have to admit that I sneaked drinks from Uncle Max's liquor cabinet, something I felt bad about doing then, and still do to this day. Which means this is my amends to them for being a little shit and a thief, and for not showing much gratitude for their love and support.

My self-centredness slowly became more pronounced as my drinking progressed. This carried over to girlfriends, and I went through them at a pretty good rate. I was a really good dancer, or so I thought, and had lots of girls who liked to dance with me. To be honest, I was more interested in impressing myself with how good I was.

Most of my performing was done at the Fire Hall and Church Hall dances, and I hung out with one of the bands a lot. The band was called "Woody's Termites" and started in our high school; they were really good. I used to jam with some with them on the drums but never actually played with them. I put this in because my kids have told people I played drums with April Wine. "Perception is truth" but in this case it just isn't. I have to set the record straight once and for all. Two members of that group went on to become original members of the band April Wine and I think Myles is still playing with them. I vaguely remember partying with them once in Waverley.

At this point I was falling deeper into my self-centredness which is the usual result of the early stages of addiction.

Some of the close calls I had when out with my friends could certainly have ended very differently. We drove our cars under the influence all the time and I wrecked two of dad's Volkswagens. I lost control on a corner and went into a ditch and then hit a culvert and flipped three times. That should have been bad but other than being sore for a few weeks I was all right.

The next crash happened while I was out drinking in Waverley and went off the road. I hit a tree which was actually very fortunate because it kept me from going into the lake. I got out of the car and made it to a friend's place and sobered up before I called dad. The next morning, we went to where I had wrecked it and dad couldn't believe how lucky I was. The tree had crushed the roof down to the floor on the back seat so a couple feet forward and I would not have walked away.

I was involved in another close call with a friend while we were out driving around in his junker having "a couple". We were coming down Meadowview Drive in Bedford which is very steep and comes out on to the Bedford highway. We lost our brakes, flew down the hill, shot out onto the highway, and went straight across into the fire hall parking lot where he finally got the emergency brake on. We also opened our doors and dragged our feet to finally get us stopped, before ending up on the railway tracks (very Fred Flintstone-like). Man, that was one crazy ride!

You would think that losing two friends to drinking and driving accidents around this would have made us more cautious, but it didn't slow us down one iota.

The nice, comfortable little safety net I thought I had woven around me ended the morning my first term marks came back for my second crack at grade eleven. My marks were an absolute joke and dad woke me up that morning with "congratulations, you are now part of the work force".

By this this time I was unable to participate in school sports because I was too old and to be honest, that was the only reason I was still going to school anyway, so on the one hand it was a relief, but it was also pretty scary. By this time, my father had caught me drinking, and probably saw the writing on the wall, so he finally started making me responsible for my actions.

I found a job cutting lines for a survey crew that surveyed the twinning of the highway up to the airport from Bedford and in the process also found a few more drinking buddies. That job was seasonal and pretty crappy so when we finished up, I got a job stocking shelves at McDonald's Save Easy in Lower Sackville, NS. During this time my drinking was becoming pretty much a daily thing. I never missed work though I did show up hung over on many occasions.

I was still playing ball, but my drinking was even starting to affect that. A few of the umpires started to ask if I had been drinking the night before and, if I admitted I had been, they said they would be on their toes. If I said no, they knew I would not let a ball get by me and no doubt felt much safer. I thought this was kind of funny, but it was also embarrassing as well.

The last school function I went to was as a spectator at the provincial track meet in Truro. I got drunk and made a complete fool out of myself. Apparently, I was aimlessly staggering around the infield. One of my friends told me he had asked me to help him mark his run- up for the long jump. Well, not being able to focus at all I ended up just wandered off, much to his disgust. By this time, I was blacking out on a regular basis, and losing friends because I was not a fun guy to be around anymore.

I also had an infected pancreas (probably from too much booze) which caused me severe pain and when I drank too much I would writhe on the ground. My friends would have to hold me down until the spasms passed. I have a few fuzzy memories of being held down and I can say that this did cause me to slow down for short period of time.

I remember hating it because I couldn't feel comfortable anywhere now. This should have pointed out how much I relied on alcohol to function, but I just couldn't see it then. THAT GUY was gradually being replaced with, "Oh God, not that guy!" That is how I felt, even though it probably wasn't totally accurate. The truth is, when not drinking I was still a pretty decent person, but the problem was there was less and less of that person as time went on. I was now avoiding social settings that did not have drinking attached to them as my obsession with drinking was gradually taking over my thought processes. The only time I felt somewhat comfortable was when I was drinking, and I started to feel most comfortable when drinking alone...

Most of our drinking was done in cars in out-of-the-way places or in someone's house but we would wear out our welcome there soon enough. Our game plan for dances was to get a bottle of wine, cheap and fast, chug it and then get into the dance quickly so we could enjoy the buzz. I was called the wine porch climber because once I got drunk on it I had no idea what I would end up doing. I hated the taste and drank it for the effect. This made me a cheap drunk.

Someone once told me a rut was a grave with both ends kicked out. It felt like that.

My brother Ted was army, and my oldest brother

Peter went to the coast guard, so we were all in one service or the other. I never told my dad, or anyone else for that matter, what I was doing until I had been accepted but I think he was glad that I had chosen to go into the navy. I had a few weeks to kill before I went to Cornwallis for basic training, so I got in as much drinking as possible.

The bootleggers got a lot of our business and you could find us in Lucasville or at Mama Pearl's on the Cobequid Rd. late at night and on weekends. Mama Pearl would not sell to us if we were too drunk, and we were such good customers she would let us run a tab until payday. This was all starting to be pretty old and boring, and my job was certainly of the dead-end variety, but all I had was a grade ten education, and even in those days you couldn't get much with that level of education. Everyone I was hanging around with was in the same boat, and I started to feel like I was stuck in a rut at the ripe old age of nineteen.

I had spent some time in the army militia while in high school and kind of liked the physical aspect of it. I also enjoyed training with weapons. I decided I would check out the regular forces, so I went in for an interview and wrote the tests to determine what trade I was suitable for.

I was accepted in June of 1968 and had to pick between Airframe technician (air force), Vehicle Technician (army) or Weapons Surface (navy). At the time I was going with a well-known car dealer's daughter, and so picked the navy as that was based in Halifax which meant I could be close to her. And besides, my dad had been navy.

My last week or so of being a civilian would have been memorable, no doubt, if I actually had any clear memories of it. I do recall almost being thrown in jail the night before I was to catch the train out to training in Cornwallis, NS. There were several nights of just drinking and they were a blur at best. Of course, I spent the rest of my time with my girlfriend. There was a dance at the church hall the night before I left, and I got pretty hammered. At the end of the dance there was a fight and it turned into a bit of a riot between the kids from Lucasville and the kids from Bedford, and I wandered through the whole thing and somehow never got hit once. I don't think I threw a punch, either.

There was a full beer bottle just lying on the ground, so I picked it up and was drinking it when the RCMP officers stopped and threw me in the car. I do remember telling them I couldn't spend the night in jail because I was catching the train for Cornwallis in the morning. For that reason alone, they let me go which was quite nice of them as I'm quite sure prior to mentioning that I'm pretty sure I was being an asshole.

That was around eleven pm or so. I didn't (literally) fall through our front door until around four later that morning. I had borrowed a friend's car to drive home.

Probably because I thought I was far too drunk to walk. My mother was sitting up waiting for me. Knitting.

Mom, God bless her, managed to pour me onto the train on time (the "Jitney," it was called, if my memory serves me) at eight in the morning, and I'll bet she was very happy to see me get on it. I quickly passed out and slept most of the way there, coming-to only when we stopped to pick up others along the way. I then stepped off the train in Cornwallis, a very sick and hungover young man, set to begin the next chapter of my life.

There were to be many roads ahead. Some more travelled than others.

4 BASIC TRAINING

My foot hit the ground and my fuzzy head was assaulted by the voice of a very angry man with a stick under his arm screaming at me to form up. Everyone was milling around and had no idea what "form up" even meant, let alone the three ranks that were expected. The harsh words and volume increased as the frustration and confusion ramped up.

Thank God I had previous exposure from my militia days, or I would probably have panicked and gotten back on the train. His job, of course, was to try to organize this rabble into some semblance of an orderly group and then, once satisfied, march us off into our service. We were a disjointed bunch. I would love to have a video of us on that first day and then compare it to our graduation parade.

I certainly was not in Kinsac or, for that matter

Kansas, anymore.

And if this was Oz, the Munchkins wore uniforms and were very, very, angry.

The next few days were filled with settling into the barracks, getting our kit and marking it up, and learning how to store everything properly. We had to put our name on every piece and were issued a stamp to use – an improvement over the days when recruits had to sew their names onto everything. We learned to roll all of our clothing and place it in a very specific way in our locker. Getting used to sleeping in a barracks with thirty some- odd guys is an experience all by itself, let alone the protocol for mass showering and the strategies involved in fighting for sink time. We had to shave every morning even if it wasn't necessary, but you didn't have to put a blade in the razor.

One of the first things we experienced was our first military haircut, basic training style. There wasn't much style involved, however, as clippers were simply put to scalp until all that was left was bristle. It took a minute at most. They probably brought guys off the sheep farm to do the job. We certainly felt like sheep being processed, but at least sheep were able to bleat their protest: we were commanded to be silent.

There were about 90 guys in our division, and I don't think it took two hours to shear the whole bunch. My hair was short before I went in, so I got off better than most. A lot of guys with longer, Beatles-style hair styles suffered the worst of all and more than a few shed some tears. If you've ever seen a dog after they've been sheared at the groomers, you know what we looked like. It took a few days to get used to this new whitewall look. I do remember a lot of laughs at one another's expense.

We also had a medical exam to go through. This is not set up with privacy in mind, so you soon lose any notion of being an individual with any rights. Perhaps that's the point. Among the many procedures involved in the medical exam was what I will delicately describe as a "short arm inspection". I'll leave that one to your imagination. Suffice it to say it's about as enjoyable as you would imagine. Though enjoyment definitely isn't the point of that.

We had our first round of shots for God knows what, and several guys got very sick from it. Some even had to be hospitalized for a few days. After a few weeks we got the next round of shots, again not really knowing what it was or what it was for. All we knew was that it was called the Five-in-One, a name I can only reason came because it contained five vaccines in one shot. We went right to the parade ground after getting it and did over an hour of a saluting drill. We all had sore arms as a result. A few got sick again.

Once we got our FNC1 rifle to drill with, we all really felt like we were now in the military. Any poor fool who referred to the rifle as a "gun" was ordered to run the parade square at high port (holding the rifle across his chest) shouting "This is my rifle, and this is my gun; this is for shooting and this for fun." My last reference to the "short arm". I promise.

All of these drills, and pretty much anything else we did, were accompanied by someone screaming at you. You were regularly told how slow, incompetent, and stupid you were, and I thanked God every day for that summer in the militia. This was all designed to break you down in order to build you back up as a military member who obeyed orders quickly and without question.

Looking at it now, I see how it gave an identity to someone who didn't feel like he had one. And for someone who always drifted on the outskirts of various groups and never really fit in anywhere, this was just what I needed to feel like I belonged.

There was so much going on all around me I didn't have time to over-think things. In the military you learn to just react to what's in front of you and this helped get me out of my head. For a period of time at least. I was told again and again not to think and to just follow orders. In a way it was like a forced vacation for my over-analytical brain. There was also very little drama among the guys I was around as it simply wouldn't be tolerated by our superiors. This is probably why I avoid it to this day if at all possible.

I guess my militia training helped me stay calm and on track. I was selected as head recruit for the first phase of training. It might have been only for a week or two, but it meant that if anything went wrong, I was responsible, so I worked my tail off and managed to keep everything running smoothly.

Thankfully, I never got reamed out too badly or too often.

I found out pretty quickly that I enjoyed the challenge of keeping everyone in line and was really feeling like I was in my element, but it did mean spending lots of extra hours keeping my kit up to standard. This required every piece of uniform to be ironed with creases just so, included your underwear. There was a picture on display of how your locker should look and yours had better match it; dust was not permitted. We used tons of spray starch, so the creases were knife-like, and the gun shirts and bell bottoms were ironed inside out which just added more difficulty.

Once I had my bed made so that it would pass muster (close inspection), I would sleep on the floor on my fire blanket. But once I was replaced as head recruit, I was able to abandon that strategy as I now had time to keep my kit up.

That first real taste of leadership awakened in me what my old report cards mentioned: that I had leadership qualities. The only difference was that now I was performing up to my potential. I also formed the foundations of my leadership style during that time, in that I prefer to lead by working alongside those in my charge, valuing their input; a style that has stayed with me throughout my working life.

Every morning there was a kit and bed inspection and the Corporals seemed to love tearing everything apart if they saw the least little thing out of place. They also seemed to love doing it just for the hell of it, as many times nothing seemed wrong to our eyes. It even went to the point of throwing mattresses out the window, the poor victim then being given just minutes to put back together what took hours to get ready the night before.

We were often pulled out of bed in the middle of the night to run the beach wearing one sneaker and one boot, or up and down Heart Break Hill until there were several guys puking. Once they achieved that level of distress, they would run us back to barracks and we would fall into a dead sleep until what felt like only minutes later when they'd be back in, smashing garbage can lids together to wake us up for the day.

Burning the pebbles off our boots and bringing them up to high shine took a tremendous amount of effort and patience. You had to heat a spoon up really hot and then burn off the rough pebbles before spending hours and hours spit-shining the shoe to get it up to where it could pass inspection. Some guys would take a short cut by using some kind of a spray, but nothing compared to a good old-fashioned spit-shine, and the sprayers always got in trouble eventually anyway.

Each person was responsible for their own kit, but

we always helped each other where we could. Some guys were good at spit-shining boots, or tying cap tally bows, or some other skill, and would help the ones who weren't as proficient. This brought the whole platoon up to standard because if one person fell short, we all shared the punishment. This taught us teamwork and gave us pride in our unit.

I got to know Cpl. Cathgard pretty well. Brendon Blaze Cathgard. The name had a ring to it; he was our platoon Cpl. and was from Cape Breton, I believe. He didn't weigh more than a hundred and fifty pounds but was made out of spring steel. He could dress you down on the parade square holding a rifle by the end of the barrel with a straight arm for minutes at a time, with the butt of the rifle right under your nose.

His arm wouldn't even shake.

If that doesn't impress you, try taking a shovel and hold it straight out in front of you by the end of the handle and see how long you last. The rifle would weigh twice that. As tough as he was, he was also a very fair and funny guy and I still think of him fondly now and then.

The rest of basic training went pretty well and, as I said before, I really excelled at the physical side of things. Since most of the punishment would include running, push-ups, or some other such activity, I managed to make out okay. Handling and firing weapons were also right in my wheelhouse. They put me at Right Marker for the division. This was the far right of the front row and I set the pace for 90 guys. If you made a mistake, it was instantly noticed. Although not the tallest, which was the normal procedure for that position, with my shorter legs I had a natural, standard, thirty-inch pace built-in, and that way everyone would stay in step. However, I'm also left-handed and would occasionally turn the wrong way which would always get me publicly reamed out.

About three or four weeks into basic training, Cpl. Cathguard told me my brother was posted to Cornwallis and would be one of my instructors. I said they wouldn't do that and bet him a case of beer it wouldn't happen. The following week my brother Ted showed up and I had to pay up on my bet.

I definitely didn't receive any breaks by having my brother there. If anything, I got it worse. The instructors would quietly come up behind me and, because I was paying attention so I wouldn't screw up, yell behind me. I would jump because I was startled. They would then get in my face because I had moved. Oh, the fun we had. It drove me to be better and made me much tougher as a result.

As we neared the end of basic training, we earned a pass so we could leave the base, and everyone took the chance to blow off some steam. If you screwed up, you lost that privilege, and many did. I would go to my brothers place and drink all his beer as a small form of payback. He lived with his wife in PMQ's on the base, so it was convenient for me and kept me out of trouble as I never went into Digby (the closest town) with my buddies.

I should mention that a few weeks into basic training I got my first and only "Dear John" letter from my girlfriend. I had joined the navy to be near her once I graduated but she dumped me anyway, shortly after I started basic training. Oh well! I was busy by then, and there was also this little Wren (female navy personnel, the WRNS) I had my eye on by the name of Rose. It's amazing how fast a heart can be mended by a single Rose.

There isn't much time for romance while going through basic training, but we did have some time at the recreation centre, dancing, and we took some nice long walks. She was a really nice girl and when I graduated, I drove back to see her as she was a couple weeks behind me in training. But that was really the end of it. We were both going in different directions, and I only saw her a couple of times after that, but she did help me get over my rejection.

The food wasn't bad and there was a lot of it, but I spent most of my pay on hotdogs at the canteen. I hated wasting time standing in the lineup for meals. By eating at the canteen, I could get back to the shack to work on whatever I needed to work on. Unlike most recruits, I think I might have finished basic training about ten pounds heavier than when I started, about one seventy-eight lbs., but it was pretty much all muscle.

I was in probably the best all round shape I would ever be in and other than the odd weekend, did very little drinking the entire time. Before graduation we had to pass the swim test which included jumping into the pool fully clothed, swimming a lap, and then treading water for a period of time. After many impromptu swims fully clothed while fishing as a kid, this test was breeze.

For our last phase I was asked to be head recruit as they wanted to get all of us working as a unit – there had been a few issues that reflected badly on our division. Their plan almost backfired because one of our guys got the crap beat out of him by someone from a junior division and, having been put in charge, I was planning a full-out attack on that division in retaliation.

However, once it was explained that we would all probably be re-coursed (doing basic over again or a minimum of extra weeks of basic training) this dampened our enthusiasm somewhat. The fact that it had been actually two guys who had a fight, and not an entire group beating up one of our guys, shone a different light on the incident and I was able to settle down and get everyone else settled down. It was a close thing, but when you get charged up with a group, reason often goes out the window and in our anger it really felt like the right thing to do.

We managed to graduate and only lost one guy who got held back. We were the first fully integrated division to graduate from Cornwallis. There were six from the air force, one army guy, Evans (funny how that name stuck with me), in our division and the rest were all navy who graduated in October of 1968. Evans being the only army guy in Cornwallis at the time didn't have a dress uniform or dress boots, so I lent him my second pair of boots for graduation and he wore fatigues (work dress) for the graduation parade. Cornwallis up to that time had been a navy training facility only.

Some of those guys I saw every now and then and one ended up being my best man when I got married a couple of years later. For some reason I had a hard time remembering his name early in basic training, so I had given him the nickname "Feather" which stuck with him long after he left the navy. I tracked him down a few years ago (he goes by Keith now) and he told me it had taken a few decades to get rid of that nickname!

Basic training was the first serious accomplishment I did on my own that I excelled at. I came out second for best all-round recruit, but my brother Ted told me I would have won if it wasn't for the fact that he was one of my instructors. They felt it would not have looked proper. I remember being strangely fine with that, and I just felt good to have done well in all areas of basic training and to have had a good reputation as a leader.

Graduation and the passing out parade were

extremely proud moments for me as this had been a far from easy transition. Basic training transformed me from a boy to (in some degree) a man, and as hard as the whole ordeal had been, I was somewhat reluctant to leave. But there was also the excitement of starting the next chapter of my life, which was a much stronger feeling.

Looking back, I can see that this period was a short break from the downward slide that I had been on. As I now know it was only a short reprieve and bore no resemblance of what was to follow. I was soon back on the train and off to CFB Halifax for my trade training in Weapons Surface and Seamanship. I had survived basic training and life was about to get much freer.

That was the real start of my navy career.

5 SHIPS AND PORTS

HMCS Stadacona (Stad), now known as "CFB Halifax", was my next destination.

For the next three months the Fleet School was my training ground and my education was mainly trade-based. While there I actually learned what I would be doing for the rest of my career. We did some maintenance, machining, electrical, mechanical and bos'n (short form of "boatswain) training. Bos'n training was a separate training phase that taught us seamanship, and which included all the equipment on the upper deck and how to rig it all (setting it up), as well as splicing rope and wire and lots and lots of knots.

We also spent quite a bit of time at Osborne Head, which was the gunnery range where we learned to maintain and fire the 3"/50 guns which most of our ships carried as their main armament. That was a lot of fun, and we would fire at targets towed by tugs or aircraft. It got a little dicey when the gun's radar locked in on the towing wire of the raydop (target) towed by the aircraft, because the rounds would track up the wire towards the plane. The water off the coast must have tons of practice rounds laying on the bottom. We would have our gunnery practice halted on occasion as some fisherman decided to take a shortcut through the range to his fishing grounds.

I had a friend of mine who used to fly the T-33 aircraft which towed our targets and he told me he got very nervous when explosions started tracking up the wire toward him. All we ever heard on the radio was "Cease fire! Cease fire! Cease fire!" and we thought it was hilarious. We were safe on the ground, after all.

Now that we had free time in the evenings and weekends, unless we pulled a duty watch, we took full advantage of the Fleet Club and there was a mess (bar) right in the barracks where we could get beer in the evenings. Can you guess who took full advantage of all that? We would shut the place down and manage to stagger, argue, or fight, our way back to our rooms just up the stairs. Fully prepared for learning the next day as I'm sure you can imagine.

At the same time, I was occasionally going back to Bedford (my old stomping grounds), and sometimes took some of my buddies with me. I continued to go to the dances and soon had another girlfriend, but since I now lived in barracks it wasn't easy to get around; I had no wheels. The training went well for me, and so did the partying. Time flew by and suddenly my training was completed, and my first ship's posting came through.

I was posted to HMCS Assiniboine, a River-class destroyer, which meant the ship was named for a Canadian river. I lived in the Weapons Mess with about fifty other guys. If I had thought it was crowded in Cornwallis, this dwarfed that situation. In the mess, we got a bunk which were stacked three high and side by side with a "buggery box" - great name - between them where we put books or other things we may have needed in a hurry, such as our gas masks and life jackets. Our lockers were less than half the size of the ones in Cornwallis, and I now knew why they stressed the importance of properly stowing our kit. There was a small settee (lounge) area where you could relax on breaks or after coming off watch and especially around tot time (rum issue).

The Navy at the time was testing a new device called the Bear Trap, which was used for hauling down the helicopters by a wire as they hovered over the flight deck, and we were looking for rough weather in which to try it out. Our ships with their higher freeboard (distance from the upper deck to the water) could take rougher sea states than the Navies of other countries. The Bear Trap would also allow us to fly in rougher weather, which made our anti-submarine capabilities very useful to NATO. That was my introduction to the sea, and I felt horrible for about three days. I didn't throw up but sure as hell felt like it (or dying, which also felt like a viable choice).

During that first week of trials, we were out with a couple of other ships and hit a real nasty piece of weather. The upper deck or "weather deck," as it was also known, was out of bounds which meant no one was allowed out there. A few of my mess mates sneaked out for a smoke and one of the guys (Wayne) was swept overboard. We never recovered him and the ships following behind us saw no sign of him either. Normally we would have turned and gone back over the area, but the seas were so high it would have endangered all of the ships to turn broadside to the huge waves. The bad weather we had sought now hindered our ability to affect the rescue. Donny (aka Twiggy) had been holding Wayne, but the "greeny" (wave) was too strong, and Wayne was torn from his grip and washed overboard.

That was how my naval career began.

I've sailed with many men over the years and have long forgotten their names, but Wayne stays in my memory. He was one of the guys who had been friendly to me when I first came onboard. I'm so thankful that we never lost anyone else during the rest of my career. That event, so early in my career, taught me that the sea is no joke and you had better be aware at all times; we are nothing but insignificant specks in comparison to the ocean.

In rough weather it was hard to get around and if it was really bad you would be "stood down," which meant you found a place that you could hang on to until it was all over. If you were a roundsman your job was to walk throughout the ship to ensure there was no loose equipment which could cause harm, and to make sure there were no leaks. If you were on watch and had to change positions at all, it was very difficult and dangerous in rough seas.

If you were forward towards the bow, just going up a ladder could be hazardous because it could feel like you weighed twice your weight, or the flip side could happen and the ship could plunge into the trough of a wave making you feel almost weightless. I know I have started climbing the ladder from 2 Mess to 1 Mess and put my foot on the bottom step of the ladder and ended up in the 1 mess when the ship dropped out from under me. It is a strange and dangerous feeling, and guys are hurt a lot in that kind of weather.

I was enjoying this lifestyle because it provided easy access to beer, and I was legally allowed to drink it at nineteen. However, I was still technically "UA" (underage) because to get the tot you had to be twenty. I was thankful that I had my birthday shortly after I joined the ship!

The tot was, If I remember correctly, two and a half ounces (or half a gill) of Pusser's Rum (Navy-speak for "purser's rum", because the purser was responsible for distributing it). The rum was, I believe, 54.5% alcohol proof and we had to mix it with pop or water at the table where they issued it, to prevent us from hoarding it. So our goal was to draw a neat one (not mixed) and get away with it, and then we could put the neat rum in an empty, thoroughly cleaned, coke can and use that for the mix in front of the officer and then start saving it up. The lineup was long, so the officer got laxer towards the end and if you were trying to hoard your rum, you lined up toward the rear of the line. Some guys were really good at saving, but I was never able to get much more than a pint before I tore into it, with predictable results.

We affectionately called it "instant stupid" or "one tot shit hot" as it really did carry a kick. It was medicinal, in that if you felt queasy it helped settle your stomach which in turn helped you to eat. It was also a great pain reliever. The tots were also a type of currency because we could charge tots, instead of money, for any job done for a shipmate or if you stood a weekend watch. We would charge up to five or more tots for a holiday watch.

When it was your birthday, a friend would be your "rum bos'n" and go around to different mess decks, collecting sippers (small splashes of rum) and then you would both get hammered. Just talking about that rum (which I haven't had in over forty-five years) makes the memory of the taste come back vividly!

A little history here about the tot.

The British Navy used it for over three hundred years to get men ready to fight or be brave enough to climb masts to unfurl sails in storms or, mainly, to keep them content with their lot in life at sea. We got rid of the tot in March 1972 (known as "Black Tot Day") and I remember that because I got drunk on tots the day before and broke my ankle sparring with another drunk sailor in the Hangar. I was so drunk they set my ankle with no pain meds because I didn't really need it as I had enough onboard as it was. I missed out on having my last tot because I was in the hospital as a result of the stuff.

While I was ashore until my ankle healed my buddy Twiggy got me a lacrosse stick when he went home for a visit. I had a walking cast on when he came home and gave me the stick. I taught myself how to use it in the storage room of the hospital and practiced by myself, just like I did as a kid, until I was proficient with it. I got the cast off one week and started playing senior lacrosse the next, this was my way of rehabbing the ankle. It was a crazy fun sport and I played it until we moved to Kentville a few years later.

The tot was also issued to celebrate exceptional performance by the crew, or when we had to work in freezing conditions for an extended time. These occurred rarely, however, and only twice in my whole career.

We had a pop machine that would randomly

dispense beer, and after so many pops a beer would come out. There were guys who would hang around when they filled the pop machine so they could gauge when the next beer would come out and believe it or not, I was not one of those guys. I did get my fair share though as some guys actually wanted pop. Strange!

The tot was issued every noon hour and would be proceeded with a pipe (announcement) of "Up Spirits Hands" to "Muster for Grog" (another term for rum) and if you were sneaky, you could get your rum at eleven-thirty with the afternoon watchmen, (those on duty at noon) who eat early and have an hour nap. At four every day they beer was issued at the canteen and they gave you two beer which you had to open there but if one was crafty, they could manage to not open those as well.

We would have bingo night and with each card bought, you got a beer with it. Up to that time I didn't realize how good a bingo player I was and was amazed at how many cards I could play, or not, as it is hard to drink and play.

For an up-and-coming alcoholic it was like Nirvana because I was surrounded by people who drank just like I did. How lucky could a guy get? As it turned out...maybe not so much.

My first trip south was a clear demonstration of what my life in the navy would be like for the next seven years or so. One of my first trips to San Juan, Puerto Rico almost ended in my death. I ran into a guy

I knew from my Bedford days and he was on the HMCS Cape Scott - our supply and maintenance vessel, which was stationed in San Juan for the duration of the Assiniboine's time down south.

We hooked up and went ashore and started drinking in all the places he had discovered. At some point during the early morning hours, I became aware of a fight and saw that it was my winger getting the crap beat out of him. My first instinct was to help but he said to stay out of it and then another guy pulled a gun and held it to his head and asked the guy who was beating on him if he wanted him dead or alive. It filtered through my alcoholic haze and instantly a clear thought came through loud and clear; if they shot him, I was the only witness so I wouldn't walk away from this either.

They decided not to shoot us and demanded any money we had, and then threw us out of the club. The sun was just coming up and we started running back to the ship and I realized I was adrift (late). We thought we heard bikes and were afraid they were coming after us, so we climbed over a fence running between the highways and kept going. During this dash for life, he told me that they were a motorcycle gang that he had been hanging out with and that he had stolen one of their jackets with their "colors". I went from fear for my life to anger at him for getting me into that situation.

We got back to where the ships were, and I heard

the blast of the foghorn, which indicated the ship was ready to slip and proceed to sea. I left my friend to fend for himself and sprinted up the gangway of the Scott and, without breaking stride, leapt across the open water between the ships because the gangway was removed. I managed to land on the quarter deck below a drop of over ten feet. Sliding on non-skid paint is not something I would choose to do ever again. Non-skid was paint used on the upper deck to prevent slipping and was basically paint mixed with sand and then applied in a thick coat. The Chief Bos'n's Mate said, "Welcome aboard, ordinary seaman MacDonald, and you better report to the Cox'n" (he was referring to the Coxswain, who was the officer responsible for routine and discipline on the ship).

I was on charge for being adrift of a ship under sailing orders and was to see the Captain for the next "defaulters" (trial). There was a lineup in the Captain's flats (the hallway outside the Captains day cabin/office), and we marched in one at a time to plead our case. You would march in to stand in front of the Captain, stand at attention, and the order "Off Caps!" would be given, which meant you stood bareheaded before the Captain as the charge was read, and then you would tell your story, which I did.

The Skipper listened to my story and then gave me a fine and seven days "birds" (punishment), which included confinement to ship and extra work. When asked if I had anything to say, I replied that I was happy to be alive to serve the punishment. When we got back to San Juan, I never got ashore again for that trip and was actually grateful about that. That was the start of various events that I managed to survive covering many parts of North America, the Caribbean Islands and, of course, Europe. If I thought surviving growing up in Kinsac was a miracle, some of these events were even more miraculous.

On another occasion, I was drunk in the old city in San Juan. It was starting to get light and I was lost so I had the bright idea to hitch a ride back to the ship. The Old City was so dangerous at the time that the police would not patrol there and I thought it was a good idea to jump in a strange car with people who didn't speak much English and ask them to drive me to the ship because I was a genius. That is exactly what I did, and I was driven back and let out by the main gate. This proved once again that God looks after fools and drunks and I definitely fit both categories.

I'm trying to keep these stories from being bigger than they were, but I can only explain things as I experienced them, or how they were related to me later. This for me was what a young sailor did, reacting to life as it played out and, man, did it play out. This is just my experience and I often imagine how many of these kinds of stories go untold.

Boston was one of my all-time favourite drinking towns, especially along Washington Street, fondly called the Combat Zone, where the Novelty and

Intermission Bars were to be found. It was a rough area and was always on the out-of-bounds list posted on the ship prior to entering port.

These out-of-bounds lists were there to try and protect us, but for us these were lists of where to find the real action. The atmosphere of these types of places was always electric: tense and exciting, because you never knew what would happen at any moment. For instance, we once staggered out of the Intermission Bar to find a guy laying on the sidewalk in a pool of blood (shot, I believe). We got out of there not knowing if whoever had done the shooting was still around. That was a little gutless, perhaps, but self-preservation takes over in those moments, and after all, he wasn't one of ours.

My friend Twiggy and I ended up closing a bar in Norfolk, Virginia by getting into a bit of an altercation. Twiggy was the nickname we gave him (typical navy humor) because he was as wide as he was tall - not really, but you get the picture. Twiggy and I were in the bar when a big guy started giving a woman a hard time, and Twiggy told him to lay off.

They both stood up and faced each other. The guy kept talking, smugly looking down and that was his mistake. Twiggy hit him so fast and so many times that he was down and out before he could even react. Twiggy was a lacrosse goalie and had the fastest reflexes I've ever seen on a human being. I don't think he ever got over the death of Wayne, and blamed himself for not hanging on, so when drinking he often had a short fuse.

The guy had a few of his friends there and I thought we were in deep shit for sure. The owner intervened and the cops showed up and shut the place down. After interviewing us and some others who witnessed it all, they let us go. We went to a pizza place and ordered a pizza that would feed a family of six, and I think we both got sick. Oh, the fun we used to have back then!

The great thing about being on board ship is that each ship had various sports teams who competed against the other ships' teams, and local teams in foreign ports, and I fit right in. I played hockey, fast ball, soccer and volleyball for the ship and we had a great time. Depending on where we went, we would play local teams in soccer and fastball and of course would follow up with lots of drinking. If it wasn't for that, I probably would have never left the dockside taverns and pubs. At least I got to see the countryside on the way to these games but was mostly out of it for the remainder of the time.

When you played for your ship there was a lot of pride and bragging rights on the line so there were no holds barred. Our Fleet Hockey Tournaments were some of the roughest hockey I ever played and, as hard as we played against each other, we partied just as hard. We competed against each other in various sports to see who would represent the fleet at the small base regionals which would have teams competing from all over the Maritimes and you could qualify for the large base regionals as well.

There was a lighter side of these sporting events where winning took a much lower priority. There was a game called "beer ball" and it was loosely played like normal ball except you had to down a beer before you could advance to the next base. If you were smart, you hit singles which gave you a little more time to drink the beer. A home run usually provided a lot of laughs (and occasionally puking was involved). I don't believe anyone actually kept score or knew when the game was done. A variation of this was "donkey ball", the only difference was that riding a donkey from base to base was added. I never personally had a chance to play that version. I may be somewhat off on the rules as clear memories are not possible from those events.

We played volleyball on the flight deck or hangar which added an element of risk since the ship could roll when you were in the air and you could end up on your back quickly. When played on the flight deck, the ball would be tied to the net to keep it from going overboard. We also played a type of cricket where you protected a square taped to the hangar door with your bat, and the ball was also tethered to prevent it from being lost. We came up with many ingenious ways to kill time when at sea for long periods. We also worked out and running on the flight deck was very difficult since you were constantly going uphill, sidehill or downhill depending on the roll. If the ship rolled sharply, you had to really pay attention or end up very quickly in the safety netting on the sides of the flight deck.

One of the guys had a set of drums that I ended up with somehow and we started a band on board which was pretty good if I do say so myself. My brother Ted was a drummer in the army band and gave me a set of drumsticks and a practice pad when I was around twelve, and I taught myself how to play. We were practicing in the hangar during an open house (ships tour) in a foreign port and were told to stop because there was a crowd forming and holding up the tour. That was something else that was important on ships -- music -- and there was a lot of good talent onboard. Whenever a few ships tied up together, I would look up my buddies from Cornwallis and go ashore together, and that always proved to be a fun time. It invariably ended with someone being carried back onboard.

We were always looking for things to bring back to the mess as trophies, like signs or things from a drinking establishment, perhaps something off their wall. We once thought bringing a hundred-pound fire hydrant cover back to ship was a fine idea until after a mile or so. When our arms felt like they were falling off, it was deemed to be not such a great idea after all. But we did it anyway. We ended up getting it all that way and then, much to our disappointment, they wouldn't let us bring it on board.

I remember hanging onto an awning once, while having a leak outside a fine establishment, and the border tore when I lost my balance and fell. We arrived back at the ship with a twenty-foot banner with the name of some eating place and it was filthy, but it hung in our mess until we were ordered to get rid of it. Most of these items were attained through stealth or stupidity (but usually more of the latter).

We had great fun whenever we came alongside our tanker to re-fuel or for a jackstay to transfer stores. Either exercise meant we were joined to the other ship by a fueling hose, or a jackstay, which is heavy line across which stores and even people are pulled over the water between the ships. These exercises are very stressful and dangerous but also a chance have some fun.

We would make grapefruit guns from spent (used) 3"/50 shell casings and they could fire a rotten grapefruit by compressed air or a charge of some kind up to a couple of hundred feet or more. We would start "shooting" after we started to break away from the other ship, and there would be teams on both sides firing at each other, and sometimes even hitting the mark. All was fair game as long as you didn't land one on the bridge where all the officers were located. There is something mesmerizing about watching a rotten grapefruit reach the top of its arc in a clear blue sky and then realize that your aim was off (or possibly not) and that the grapefruit was headed for the bridge. There was an immense amount of satisfaction watching officers scramble for cover; the blast of shit you were to receive was often more than worth it.

One of our ideas (which sounded good in theory) was to load the mortars -- large tubes used to shoot depth charges -- with garbage in plastic bags and fire those at the other ship. Reality turned out to be very different from the plan. It did fire the garbage well enough, but the plastic melted inside the barrels of the mortars and was not easily removed. The Weapons Officer was not pleased, and that turned out to be a one-time venture. Some of the grapefruit guns were works of art and ingenuity and the getups the teams wore would make the Pirates of the Caribbean proud.

I lost count of the number of times I went to Bermuda and Boston in those early years. We transited through the Bermuda Triangle many times but saw no aliens. We did, however, have a strange occurrence when we tangled with a waterspout, which is basically just a tornado of water. We were sailing through a squall (fast storm) of heavy rain when all of a sudden, the ship heeled (tipped) over to a forty-five-degree angle or more, and all the air was sucked out of the ship. It lasted well less than a minute and we righted ourselves and the air returned to normal, but it scared the crap out of us. There were several broken bones and nasty falls, and one guy had to be flown off the ship due to an injury and mental breakdown as he had been on the upper deck and was almost washed overboard.

Bermuda is an amazing and beautiful island. It is also hard on the body, as so many sailors can attest. You can rent Mopeds to get around which is the best way to see the island, but they drive on the "other side" of the road and the roads are very narrow. If you're sober this can be dealt with easily, but if you are drunk... not so much. Most of the roads are bordered by walls of coral and when you scrape along those, they will peel your skin off and then quickly get infected. Canadian sailors would have to pay three times the normal deposit because the renters were tired of fishing the bikes out of the water at the end of the jetty (pier) or having them returned completely wrecked. When we sailed from there, it would often look like some of crew had been in a war zone.

The island has some wonderful beaches and when I could pull myself away from the NAFFI Club, I spent time swimming and snorkeling. It is such a small speck in the Atlantic, in the middle of the Gulf Stream which gives it the tropical climate. How the old mariners managed to find it is beyond me, as even with all our modern equipment we managed to miss it on occasion.

There is a fair amount of down-time when you are at sea. It's scattered between your watches which were broken up in seven parts so that your rotation was staggered, and your sleep patterns would be screwed up until you got back home. Sailors are notoriously big readers and I was no exception. We played a lot of card games and some board games but for a lot of guys it was just shooting the shit and drinking. You knew better than to be drunk on watch because that was not tolerated but hung over was okay, even though it made the watch much harder for sure.

During your watch, you would rotate positions every hour between wheelhouse, port and starboard look out, life-buoy sentry, bridge and spare. I'm digging in my brain back to 1968 to '74 and I may be off a little on the names so any help from my readers would be appreciated. I always disliked life-buoy sentry as you were on the quarter deck all by yourself, making sure you were alert enough to throw a lifebuoy (also known as a "kisbee ring") to anyone who fell overboard. It was creepy as hell at night as chains rattled, and the wind moaned, and you started seeing all kinds of things that weren't there. Your relief would often scare the crap out of you when you were running in a darken ship protocol (no lights), if you didn't see him open the door.

We would have exercises with other ships where we would run silent and try to find each other. We'd fire star shells which would float down on parachutes and light up the other vessel. We were in a heavy fog at dusk one day and I saw a light in the sky and thought we had been found. I soon realized it was the masthead light of the other ship which was coming right at us. The quick action of both Officers of the watch prevented a horrendous collision. The guys on the Quarterdeck said they could have stepped across to the other ship. That's how close we came.

Shortly after putting to sea on a grey overcast October morning in 1969 I was on lookout on the bridge wings, just off the English coast, and I reported a plume of smoke off the starboard bow. Within minutes we discovered that it was smoke from an explosion on HMCS Kootenay. They just had, the fiftieth anniversary of that horrendous event. We diverted to lend aid and had some of our damage control guys go over to help. There had been a gearbox explosion in the engine room and a fire ball traveled down the flats. Between the explosion and the fireball there were a lot of injuries and fatalities. I knew a few guys onboard and they would later tell me it was hell on earth. The ship was towed back to England and we continued home a very shaken crew. The aftermath of that explosion caused a lot of what is now known as PTSD but wasn't really recognized as such back then. There was no counselling as we know it today, and a fair number of suicides resulted from that event, as well.

It was the worst loss in the Canadian Navy since the war.

There were good times and bad times, but this was the navy at the time. We would often jokingly say "Rest easy, Canada, your navy is on patrol". From what I have written so far and experienced I think Canada had a lot to be concerned about during the Cold War years. I personally sailed this way for many years and visited many places. I am so grateful that I spent the last fourteen years of my career sailing sober, so I got to really see the places I missed the first couple times around. Some of those places I never visited again so I definitely missed out during my drinking days.

Sailing certainly wasn't for everyone and many found that they just couldn't do it due to chronic sea sickness, time away from family, lack of privacy, or many other reasons. But for me as a young single man (and practicing alcoholic) it was glorious, and I loved every minute of it.

06 BACK HOME

One guy I got along with really well onboard was a cook by the name of Jim. He fit right in with us. Very soon it became Jim, Feather, and I, and we became close running mates for the next few years. It was at this time that we started hanging out at my old house in Kinsac. Dad had moved to Newfoundland to be the director of ship building and repair for the government right around the time I joined the Navy. Mom joined him permanently once they had everything settled, which meant they were living full time in Newfoundland by that time. As a result, they let me to "look after" the house. Looking back now, I honestly think that could be the only stupid thing my father ever did during his many years of sobriety.

To say the house in Kinsac was a party place would be a gross understatement of how bad it became.

Feather, Jim, and I, stayed there for I can't remember how long -- it's all pretty much a blur. I didn't remember dealing with snow so it must have been something like six months or so, but again I'm just not sure. We had the drums set up permanently in the living room, and a few of our friends would drop by anytime and we would drink and jam all night.

In a short period of time, the old house in Kinsac became the place to be if you wanted to party, or just to crash. I can't recall if any of my Kinsac friends hung out with us, but I'm sure some of them may have done. If any of them read this, I'm sure they could flesh out this timeline. I think in retrospect it is truly amazing that the old place remained, for the most part, undamaged because there definitely was no TLC shown it. I couldn't begin to tell you everyone who passed through that house during that time, but I have no doubt they would all have stories to tell. I will attempt to recall some adventures from that time but, as I said earlier, it was pretty much a blur.

There were stretches when we would sober up a little and realize we had no food in the house, just booze. I vaguely remember bumming a loaf of frozen bread and some mayonnaise from the neighbour across the road, and that was probably all that we ate that day. I think the only thing keeping us alive was the food we ate on board ship at noon, and any fast food we picked up on the run. I can visualize the kitchen with boxes of empties stacked to the ceiling, which we would then return so we could buy more booze.

See how responsible we were back in the day, we actually recycled.

We would sober up by going to the lake and swimming in the cold water, but it was almost pointless because we'd head right back out and get back at it again. Going to the lake was about the only thing we did that felt like my old life, but even that was usually under the influence of alcohol, or a bad hangover.

I do remember Feather and I coming to one morning surrounded by trees. We didn't have a clue where we were. It turned out I had pulled into a log road because I guess I got tired. The crazy thing was the log road was only half a mile from the house. Hazy days.

I was on duty one day and dad paid a surprise visit to check up on me. Feather and Jim were there and were both quite drunk. When Feather saw dad, he said something to the effect of "Come on in! After all it's your fucking house". Only Feather could say that to my father and live to tell the tale, but I heard about it and was quickly told we needed to clean up our act. Thankfully he hadn't seen the few holes we'd put in the walls, since we'd at least had the clarity of mind to hang things over them. Otherwise, I'm sure he would have kicked our asses to the curb long before he did.

Dad had to go to Saint John, NB for work which

was why he had come home. Feather and I got the idea to visit Feather's home in Sussex, so we got Dad to drop us off on the way. I met his family and friends and ended up getting so drunk that we went back to his place and I passed out. I opened my eyes to his mother standing over me panicking because the couch was on fire. I had passed out with a lit cigarette in my hand.

I could have caused a serious house fire, just as my father had done years before, but thankfully all I ended up doing was burning my own back a bit and ruining their couch. I can't for the life of me remember if I paid for the repair; if not, perhaps this will count as another amends made.

It was a strange thing though because when I got my wits about me, I remember saying that Feather was in trouble. I made his mother drive me around looking for him and I somehow directed her to where he was parked on a side road with a girl. In retrospect I guess the only trouble he was in was that he might have gotten her in trouble. I have no idea how I located him given the state I was in, but it was a strange event all round for sure. Dad picked us up a couple days later and it was a quiet, hungover, drive all the way back home.

It was a while after that when a buddy of ours named Corey was killed coming back to the house after driving someone home in the morning. He was an amazing guitar player and sounded just like Jimmy

Hendrix when he played Purple Haze. More importantly, he was a hell of a nice guy and a fun guy to hang out with. The accident happened on National Drug Hill which has a sharp corner at the top, with a huge pine tree and a sharp drop off; maybe a quarter mile from the house. As kids we coasted down that hill in the winter, but that is not what I think of when I drive out there now.

I was passed out at the time and didn't realize what had happened until I regained consciousness hours later, but by that time everything was over. I was at sea for his funeral, but Jim and Feather were able to go and told me all about it. The house just never felt right after that. It was probably for the best that after that sad event, dad ended up selling the house. The accident and Corey's death were the last straw. Dad didn't do it because he wanted to. I think it was an attempt to keep me alive.

You can probably tell by now that I was a very uncaring, selfish, young man at this point who had no regard for anything or anybody. I remember thinking at the time that I had it all. In some ways I might actually have had it, but in my stupidity, I squandered it all away. If I had shown good stewardship of the house and property, it probably would have been mine, because I believe dad was really sad to see it go. But what choice did I give him?

My brother Peter, who lived next door, would also drop in from time to time and have a few pops with us. I know my sister-in-law was relieved when the house was sold. She was nervous of what might happen and rightfully so. I also have no doubt the neighbours were very happy to see us go.

I was talking to my cousin the other day and she told me that she had heard there were couples "copulating" on the lawn. To be honest, given the crowd that would find their way to the house, I would say that it's definitely a possibility. But I don't recall any incidents of that nature. Thankfully my overall recall for that time period is somewhat shaky to say the least.

Would that be considered plausible deniability?

One other memory that sticks out from this period was when we bought a car from one of our friends for, I think, twenty bucks. It's possible we might still owe him for it but who knows? It was a 1959 Pontiac Star Chief that was very, very, tired. We literally ran it into the ground, and it died alongside the road one night on the way into Halifax. We walked away and left it. But while we had it, I can assure you that we used it to the limit. As it deteriorated, we celebrated the slow demise by showcasing all its faults.

Near the end of its life we would pull into the bowling alley in Bedford and the brakes would be squealing and the trunk would pop up as we cruised in. Jim would open one back door and throw out a cement block attached to the car by a rope while Feather would jump out the passenger side, lift the hood and pull off the distributor wire to shut it off. We had lost the keys. I would then open the driver's door and get out while Jim got out the other back door. We'd go into the bowling alley and there it would sit with all its doors open, trunk and hood up and still smoking with the finishing touch, the cement anchor. The Bowling Alley was where we hung out a lot of the time and was the staging ground for our various exploits. We did also bowl sometimes.

This wreck of a car was where we did a lot of our partying and as a result it did end up in the odd ditch. One night we were coming from the bootleggers and a cop started to turn around to follow us, so I floored it and got ahead enough to turn down a side street at speed. The turn was too sharp and although we made it a bit up the road we ended up in a deep ditch. Fortunately for us the case of beer we had with us ended up on top of Jim, unbroken. The lights went out and the cop passed by without spotting us. Some people helped push us out and off we went without a muffler.

I narrowly missed the law that night but wasn't so lucky on another occasion. One particular day after our nightly partying I was heading into Bedford and got pulled over by the cops. He asked if I was drinking or had any booze in the car. Miraculously, I happened to be sober at the time and was pretty smug until the cop reached in and pulled out a quart of beer from what I thought were empty boxes. I was more shocked that we had somehow missed a full bottle of beer than anything else. It was very unlike us. I ended up claiming it and got an illegal possession charge. One of my friends went to court and paid the fine as I was at sea again. I think it was under twenty bucks.

I had a new muffler put on after our visit with the ditch, and one morning I woke up to the sound of hammering. Jim was punching holes in the new muffler to make her "sound better". That was the first and last repair we ever did on the old girl. These are just a few examples of our escapades with the old Pontiac before she died and was so unceremoniously abandoned.

I often wonder why ships and cars are so often referred to in the feminine.

After the old Pontiac had breathed her last breath, Feather managed to get his mother's '58 Studebaker Golden Hawk. I think that was the name. If it wasn't someone should use it. It was a cool looking set of wheels and we put it through the paces while we had it for sure.

We were always short of money for essentials like food and gas. One day we had no gas and wanted to go into Bedford. My brother Pete worked for the Coast Guard and for some unknown reason had five gallons of "avgas" in his possession, which is aircraft fuel. We poured that in the old Hawk and off we went. We stopped where the Beaver Bank road hit the Sackville highway, and waited as there was a car coming from the other direction. Feather told me we could beat him so I floored it, but the car didn't move. He yelled for me to floor it again and I yelled back that I already had it pegged. Then the tires suddenly grabbed, and we took off in a huge cloud of smoke.

The avgas was so powerful that the tires were spinning but not even squealing, similar to a burn-out at drag race but not common for the old Studebaker to be sure. By the time we got to Bedford the valves were knocking something awful and the poor old thing needed a bit of work before he took it back to his mother in Sussex. I don't know what test the avgas was but I'm sure it was way over any high test in the gas stations and burned way too hot for the valves.

One time I got off duty and hitched a ride out to the house. Feather and Jim weren't there, so one of the guys who was crashing there took me out to look for them. We started by checking all the drinking places and eventually found the car on a back road where we often parked to drink. They weren't in the car. I got out and I could hear voices coming from the woods, so I just told my buddy to head back home.

I made my way through the wood towards the voices and came out to a small lake. The two of them were drunk as nits sitting on an old piece of plywood. When I sat down to join them the wood broke and they cried and got mad at me because I broke their bench. I remember that well because one, I was sober and two, I had to listen to them gripe all the way home.

Drunks are so sensible are they not?

I also happened to be sober when Jim and Feather came stumbling home one night completely hammered. I had just gotten off duty and arrived home late and had crashed on the couch. When they came in, Jim's face was a mess. All he kept saying was that I should have been there because they'd just been in an awesome fight. I remember thinking that it wasn't such an awesome fight at all by the look of him. I helped him get cleaned up and then he crashed. The next morning, I think he realized that it wasn't such an awesome fight after all when he looked in the mirror.

We were pretty much drinking all the time at that point. It was around this time I actually began drinking myself sober, if that's even possible. It only happened once or twice but I do remember short periods of clarity, or what I took to be clarity, in the midst of all that haze. Maybe it was a new kind of sober. I certainly don't think I would have passed a breathalyzer during those brief periods of clarity. I do remember that the hangovers after those episodes were some of the worst I have ever experienced.

I also vaguely remember a time when I was drunk for such an extended period that I was talking but couldn't seem to make sense of the words coming out of my own mouth. It was utter gibberish. This did sort of concern me for a few minutes, as it would for anyone, I'm sure, but my concern was short lived as I couldn't retain a thought for long in those days.

I guess I would say that at that time I was a full-blown alcoholic, but that even with all of the craziness surrounding me I thought of myself as a fun drunk. Basically, I was holding up my end of the stereotypical image of a "sailor" and I managed to keep that persona going for a few more years.

It wasn't long before the house in Kinsac was very much in the past and I had embraced the life of a sailor living aboard ship and hanging out at the Fleet Club where I had a locker and stored my civilian clothing. One night we all got dressed up in the new suits we had picked out at Harrods in England and went ashore. Leaving the fleet club lockers was the last clear memory I have of that night because we got into our duty-free bottles we had stashed in our lockers.

I woke up the next morning and saw bars and thought, "Nah, couldn't be", and then fell back to sleep. I woke up again only to find that the bars were real. I was in jail and looked a mess. My nice new suit was all torn and I was scraped up, bruised, and sore with no memory of how any of this came about.

I don't know how long I stayed there before an officer from the ship arrived and we went to court. I was charged with drunk and disorderly conduct in a public place, so I plead guilty and the officer paid my fine. The officer working the desk where we paid the fine asked me if I remembered what had happened and when I said I didn't, he said, "good, and I'm not telling you either". To this day I don't know what happened that got me thrown in jail. And that, my friends, is a creepy feeling.

Robin Williams once said, "blackouts are the brain's way of going into witness protection".

At this point "THAT GUY" was starting to unravel but I couldn't yet see it.

That situation could have been so much worse because while in a blackout your body is doing all kinds of things and you have no conscious memory of it. I could have done anything. Later on, while working with parole groups I heard stories of the crimes that were committed while in blackouts which led to incarceration. I would like to say that this was the only time I was thrown in jail, but it happened another time and really could have happened on many more occasions, but I was somehow lucky enough to avoid being caught.

I easily could have been one of those habitual drunk drivers who keeps getting caught and never learns the lesson. The things we borrowed and never returned could have been chargeable offences as well. I know I smuggled booze out of the dockyard many times in my hockey gear as I knew no one in their right mind would open up that bag. You're not thinking rationally while under the influence and end up doing some of the stupidest things while in blackouts.

Blackouts were also just plain embarrassing. I went to the Fleet Club one night and a girl came up to me and started talking to me. After a minute she stopped and asked, "You don't remember me from last night, do you?" I had to admit that I didn't. She then proceeded to tell me in great detail all the ridiculous things I had said to her the night before as I was hitting on her. She was kind of cute, but I couldn't look her in the eye after hearing all the utter nonsense I had said to her. All I could do was hope she wouldn't spread around how smooth I was and thank God she took pity on me and was much kinder than I probably would have been.

The Fleet Club was where the action was, and we all went there to start off the night and often finished it there as well. Of course, we primed ourselves on the cheap booze aboard ship first. Ten cents for a shot, and a quarter for a beer, is hard to compete with but for action it was the "Fleeters" (Fleet Club). The Fleet Club always had great bands and the dances were awesome. It really was the centre of our social life and was a place to go for those who lived on board ship. There were lots of guys from all over the country who had nowhere else to hang out so that was it. That is also where we had our Ships Company Dances and they were fantastic with a spread of food that was amazing. That place really knew how to put on a function.

After the house was sold, that place and that life was all I had, and at the time it suited me just fine. We were foot loose and fancy free. But just like so many other times in my life, just when I thought things were exactly the way I wanted them fate would step in and throw a wrench into the works. Little did I know at the time that a major change was right around the corner.

I also wasn't quite done with Kinsac after all, and I would re-surface there again several years later. And Karma, as we all know from experience, can be a real bitch.

7 HOOK, LINE AND SINKER

One night we all got dressed up and went to a new club called the Razzle Dazzle Discotheque, at Scotia Square in Halifax. This night was significant, not because of the amount of drinking we did but because this is where I met Judy, my wife-to-be. Jim's ex-wife was there that night as well, which was also significant since he'd never mentioned having been married to her. So, at the beginning of the evening I was the go-between for the two of them. This sucked for many reasons but mostly because Judy saw me talking to this woman and figured that she was either my wife or my girlfriend.

It took me longer to see her, but then she's always been quicker than me. I finally noticed the two girls sitting together and one of them really caught my eye. She was very beautiful but also had a wholesome look which I was drawn too. The low-cut dress she had on may also have drawn my eye a bit -- I'm nothing if not honest -- and I could see she had come from a place of good, healthy, air.

Now, being only lightly into the suds at that point I was still very capable of being THAT GUY, so I quickly went over and asked her to dance. We seemed to hit it off immediately and as the night was wearing down I asked, her "how do you ask to take someone home who has her own car?" and she replied, "I don't know, why don't you try". So, I did. One of my other friends was trying to hook up with Judy's friend so Judy first dropped her friend off (to relieve her friend of my buddy's drunken advances) and then dropped him off at the Dockyard.

I went back to her place and we talked for a long time. I believe that very early on I shared my plan of not getting married until I was twenty-six, and some other nonsense, then I left and caught a cab back to the ship. It's funny because I can still remember waiting outside her place for the cab, kicking rocks and thinking how much I really liked her. We sailed for a couple of weeks shortly after that night, and she'd thought I'd moved on, but I called her when I got back in and we started going out.

There was a bit of a glitch of course, but by then there usually was. I was also interested in another girl at this time and I didn't know which one I should go out with. I asked my buddy Feather what he thought, and he sagely asked me which one had a car. The answer to that was Judy and to this day we say that it was her Chevy Nova that sealed the deal. But to be honest she was too damn cute to ignore.

We started spending most of our free time together going to the Fleet Club dances and shows, and parking (a lot of parking). We were parked outside the Centre Gate to the dockyard one night sharing some quality time when a knock came at the window and a police officer was standing there. I rolled down the window and when he started to ask us what we were doing and I said, "Hi, Jim!". It was a guy I had gone to school with. We chatted for a while and I told him I was just saying goodnight before going into the dockyard. He smiled and left us alone. I think this embarrassed Judy a little, but I got a kick out of the whole thing.

One day she took me over to meet her father and to watch her brother play hockey at the Dartmouth rink. Her brother was playing Junior A hockey for the Dartmouth Lakers I think, and he turned out to be a really good player; not that I was paying much attention. I was working much too hard to appear sober. She told me after she'd picked me up that she noticed I had been drinking (imagine that) and out of the blue she said I had spun a tale that I had a daughter by someone in Montreal. I really don't remember that nonsensical exchange and I don't remember much about meeting her father either, to be truthful.

She invited me home to Kentville to meet her

mother after that. When she came to pick me up from the ship, I was passed out and they couldn't get me up. To say she was angry would be putting it lightly. She told me she drove faster than normal that day in the hopes that maybe she could pick up a cop on the way! My track record was not exactly endearing me to her family, and I was embarrassed but talked my way out of it somewhat, and even managed to behave a little better for a short period of time. We were young and in love and so we were willing to overlook a lot of things. Well, it was mostly Judy overlooking flaws in me, because compared to me she was already a saint in training.

I worked hard at turning her head and showing her how cool it was to be with me. As I said previously, the Fleet Club had a lot of action going on so I would take her to the dances and she really enjoyed that atmosphere. I took her to a Ship's Company Dance, and she was impressed with how nicely everything was put on and really enjoyed herself. She got to meet a lot of the guys I hung out with on the ship and there was no shortage of characters on that ship (and around the Fleet Club in general) who she got to see perform. It was always entertaining there, and we did have a lot of good times in those early years. I know she was hit on by a few guys when she was waiting to pick me up there, but I never had to worry about her.

A funny thing happened around this time which showed how ingrained my mind had become to my drinking patterns. We were visiting my brother Pete in Kinsac and we ran out of beer, so he asked me to go down and pick up a case for him. Judy and I hopped in the car and drove to the bootleggers to pick up the beer. This was Judy's first bootlegger run and we did all the old routine like sitting with lights out and the engine running while I went in and got the goods.

When we got back, Pete asked how much it was and when I told him he asked me where in the hell we went. I told him the bootleggers and he proceeded to tell me there was a liquor store right there on the same corner where I turned in to go to the bootleggers. I was so used to going there to get booze I had never even thought of going anywhere else.

In my defence, it was a new store.

We ended up taking a trip to New Hampshire to visit Judy's relatives about five months into our relationship. I proposed to her while we were there, and she accepted! But if she wasn't picking up the clues from my behaviour, her mother Marion certainly was and shared how disappointed she was in us getting engaged when we told her the news. This dampened our joy considerably. Fortunately, my parents were happy for us, perhaps hoping it would settle me down some.

Judy's mother had told her to never get involved with a sailor, a Catholic, or a drinker and I fit quite snugly into all three categories. All it did, really, was to harden our resolve and we were going to do what we wanted, regardless. The drive back from the States was unpleasant because we knew we were going to have to face her mother upon our return. Since her mom's sister had married a Catholic, and that's who we were visiting, Marion thought the whole thing was some kind of a Catholic conspiracy.

When we got home, we went directly to Judy's parents and her mother never even asked to see her ring. I sat in the living-room biting my tongue until I could no longer contain myself and finally blurted out, "I think December is a good time for the wedding." (We met in March and this was August). Marion said, "She is not twenty-one yet and I won't give my permission". I replied, "Fine. We will wait until her birthday in March and then we won't need your permission." I'm not sure but I think we left shortly after that.

But before we left, Judy's father Frank pulled her aside and told her that if she loved me, she should do what she felt was right for her.

As you can see, Marion and I didn't hit it off very well from the start and it would be many years before we were able to see eye to eye. She was doing her best to protect her daughter and could see I had issues, so I held nothing against her. Her nickname was "old white eyes" because she could see things that others missed; though you really didn't need second sight to see that I had a problem.

A few weeks later we went to a house party and

after we dropped Judy off, Feather cracked a bottle of whiskey and we polished it off while heading back to the dockyard. The car broke down by the Willow Tree in Halifax by the Commons and we couldn't get it going. By this time the whiskey had really kicked in. A cop stopped to see what was going on and apparently, I asked if he could give us a jump start.

Well, he gave us a jump start all right because shortly afterwards we were in jail and I was being charged with a DUI. This was the start of Labor Day weekend and oh yeah, I was supposed to be going home with Judy that weekend. They let Feather out in the morning, but it took a day for him to scratch up the bail money for me. When I finally got out, I grabbed a few things from the ship and started hitchhiking to Kentville. I was sick and hungover and probably should have stayed put but I couldn't let this happen again.

A guy picked me up and when I climbed into the vehicle, I saw that he had an open case of beer on the front seat. What luck! He dropped me off in Windsor and by that time I was half drunk again. I called Judy and filled her in on what had happened, and she came and got me. She told her parents what had happened before she left and when I got to her place, I was so embarrassed I went upstairs and went to bed. I kept a very low profile for the rest of our stay. Judy's mom must have thought that Judy had made quite a catch.

Thank God that was my last trip to jail, but certainly

not due to lack of trying.

When I went to court, the judge said my breathalyzer reading was .234 and that I should have been dead or at least passed out. It showed how little he knew about alcoholics because there is no doubt that I was a full-fledged member of that unfortunate club by this time. Later, I would give breathalyzer tests in detox and have seen guys blow as much as .4 and still be functioning.

As a result of all this, for the next year Judy had to drive me to work from Lucasville where we had purchased a mobile home a few months before our wedding. We thought we were really something with the mobile home -- all grown up -- but we were little more than kids. Timber Trails Trailer Park was our home for the first couple of years of our married life. The park is still there, and I drove by it just a month ago.

We had a lot of growing up to do but we had a lot fun living out there.

After we were married, Feather and Jim each stayed with us for a time and that made for some adventures on a few occasions. It was not a party house like the one in Kinsac because I was trying to be a grown-up and Judy wouldn't have put up with that nonsense anyway. I think we paid something like $7,000 for the trailer and we could just manage our expenses with both salaries.

About a month before our wedding I sailed to

Bermuda on a shakedown cruise (where the performance of a ship is tested) because we had been in refit for the last several months. While there the boys had a stag party for me at the Horse and Buggy pub in Hamilton. We were having a great time until a ruckus started, and we went outside to make sure it wasn't one of ours. It wasn't.

For some reason, however, after we went back in one of the locals wanted to pick a fight with me. I was having such a good time and tried to avoid it. I really did. But he had other ideas and wouldn't stop getting in my face and when we got up to leave, he followed us out. I must have blacked out about then because I have no recollection of what followed. Twiggy was with me and another buddy, Sammy, who was shore patrol that night. They filled me in on the following events.

As I was walking away, the guy kept yapping at me and started calling all of us cowards. Apparently, that's what caused me to turn around and go back. He kept yapping and started poking me in the chest. I responded by knocking him out cold. Then I guess I wanted to stomp him, but the boys hustled me out of there. I was told afterwards that there was a bit of a riot that followed. Before going ashore, we had been told that racial tensions were very high in that area, and to act accordingly. This made the situation even worse and particularly damaging for me as I had technically gone against orders.

I also broke my hand on that punch but didn't get a cast on it until the next day. When I regained consciousness, I had no idea what had happened until the boys filled me in. I had to have the cast put on at the local hospital and was so hungover they could have removed the hand and I would not have cared.

Once again, I was on charge and when I had to give my official side of the story, I told the skipper that I was walking away until he called the Canadian Navy gutless cowards and that was when I reacted. It was loosely based on truth which is how the best lies are crafted. He asked me if I gave as good as I got and I said, "Yes, sir. I definitely did". Based on that somewhat truthful tale, I had my case dismissed.

There is an upside -- if you could call it that -- because I now had a cast on and I couldn't work my regular job, so they put me in the laundry. Now, working in the laundry sounds like a shitty job and it was as we were washing everyone's bedding and pressing it all but here is where the upside came in: when you did someone's personal laundry, you could charge money or, better yet, tot's; you can you figure out who was pretty much drunk all the way home.

Judy and mom met the ship and when my mother saw my cast and learned how it had happened, she peeled me out in the main cafeteria in front of everyone. I remember thinking how nice it would be to be a cockroach on the floor so I could disappear down a crack. I might have gotten away with it from the captain, but my mother was a much higher authority and her words hurt more than any punishment I could have received from him.

I had the cast on for about three weeks but promised mom I would have it off by the time of the wedding, even if I cut it off myself. I went to the hospital and explained the situation to the doctor. He didn't want to take it off but after some major begging he said he would but on one condition. He put a pencil in my hand and said that if I could keep him from taking it, he would be okay with the cast coming off. He then cut it off and gave me the pencil and even though it hurt like hell and I was sweating bullets the whole time, he never got it out of my hand. What can I say? I was determined not to disappoint Judy and mom.

We got married on December 18th, 1970 -- the day after my twenty-second birthday. This makes it easy to remember and also means I really have no excuse for forgetting our anniversary. Judy was beautiful and Feather and I looked... dapper (sharp) in our brand-new green uniforms. Ugh! I hated those green uniforms but didn't have much choice because my old one was well-worn and pretty beat up. In retrospect I wish I had worn the old one.

It was really easy to tell each service apart when we all wore our individual uniforms. There was always spirited interaction between services prior to the green uniforms and you at least knew who to throw a punch at. This was now more difficult and hat badges and small lapel pins are hard to pick up when rolling on the floor. Maybe this was the idea of unification. Bad idea. None of us liked them and I referred to them as seven-up salesman uniforms because they were the same colour as the guys who drove 7-up trucks.

The night before the wedding we had a jam session and I got a little bit drunk, but not loaded. The day of the wedding I was allowed to have two beer, just to help with the hangover, and I know Marion was having us monitored. We had the ceremony at St. James Anglican Church in Kentville, and the reception at the Paramount Motel in Wolfville which was, believe it or not, a dry reception! Like I said before, Marion read the clues very well and made sure the wedding was memorable for all the right reasons.

I remember standing with Rev. Mosher off in the side room and him making a quip that there was still time to run. I wonder if Marion had a word with him knowing my record of not showing when I was supposed to. I know she wasn't a fan, but I don't think she would have gone that far.

We left the reception and got in the Volkswagen that dad had given us. He had purchased Judy's Nova, basically because we were poor. Judy had to drive as I still didn't have a license, but I was kept busy scraping the windshield so she could see. The gas heater didn't work, and we were driving in the middle of a snowstorm. We went back to the trailer and mom and dad visited the next day.

Romance was my middle name, don't you think?

Two weeks later I sailed south for a few months and we were really not prepared for that. Judy wanted me home and I wanted to be home so one night while drinking I told her to write a desperate letter and maybe I could get home for compassionate reasons. The funny thing is that when I got the letter a while later, I didn't remember telling her to write it in the first place, so my reaction was no doubt very real. It got me home a few weeks ahead of the ship.

The navy doesn't look favourably to this kind of thing and we had to go see a case worker by the name of Miss Casey. She basically told Judy that the Navy came first and that she had better get a grip and grow up. Judy looked at her and asked if she was married. When Miss Casey said no, Judy got up and walked out. I didn't see that coming. Early on in our marriage it seemed that Judy had a solid 'pair' (and me not so much). When the ship got back, we did settle into a routine which helped carry us for the next twenty years or so.

We had some growing up to do and were having the odd growing moments. Like the time I pissed her off so much she threw a plant at me and I just ducked and laughed, and she ended up cleaning it up. Another time we were in a heated discussion and she went to the bedroom and slammed the door, so I threatened to remove all the doors. One winter night again I made her so mad she left and got the Volkswagen stuck in the snow. I went out and lifted it out so she could leave. The common thread was I was the instigator to all of our spats, a pattern which would grow worse as time went on. The self-centred little shit had gotten older, but no wiser.

In March of 1972 our first child Jennifer was born, and we were now parents. Who would have thought? I was a dad who was still pretty much a kid himself. Judy and I were still trying to figure out this marriage thing and we had now just added another human being to the picture. Judy was much more prepared for this than I was.

She was thirty hours in labour and at one point I threatened the doctor that if they didn't do something for her, I was not going to be responsible for what would happen. I think my actual words were "get the fuck in here and help her or you'll be cleaning up the blood and guts". I was about to lose my shit. In those days, husbands didn't go in for the delivery which is very stressful, since you're completely helpless and the unknown eats at your mind. I remember seeing Jennifer for the first time and she had lots of black hair and coal black eyes and was so beautiful. I also remember several months later rocking her and watching Canada playing Russia when they won the Series in Russia.

When Feather was staying with us it was fairly common that he would arrive on his bike and be drunk out of his mind. I would know he was drunk when we would hear the motorcycle sitting and idling in the driveway. I would go out and hold the bike for him so he could get off and crawl into the trailer. I'd then turn it off and set it on its kickstand and follow him in to guide him into bed. One day when he landed drunk, he had no helmet and when we asked where it was, he said that he had been doing about a hundred (miles per hour people this was the seventies) and it just popped off his head. We went back to find it, but he had no idea where it happened, and he kept falling into the ditch looking for it.

Jim was staying with us one night when we had an incident with beer... imagine that! I was making my own home brew because we were poor, and I was cheap, but it was pretty good (in that it carried quite a kick). We had a batch put up and I must have added too much sugar, or it was too warm where it was fermenting because in the middle of the night, we heard a pop. At first, we thought Jim had broken a light bulb but shortly after we heard a few more pops. When we went to investigate, we saw liquid running out from under the door where the home brew was stored.

They were exploding. We took them out with gloves on and started popping the tops, causing beer to shoot up to the ceiling. It was an absolute mess. And that, my friends, was the last home brew ever to be attempted in our home.

Just before the home brew debacle, Judy's young cousin from the States came for a visit. Like a lot of young men, he had an over-inflated view of his capabilities when it came to drinking. I offered him a brew and he took it, chugged it and said it wasn't bad. I warned him it was pretty strong, and he told me about drinking a case once, by himself, and being able to handle it. I gave him another and he chugged it as well. When he asked for another, I said no. He promised me he would nurse it if I gave him one more so after some assurances I did. He was good on his promise and he really was taking it slow when he felt a bit ill and went outside to be sick.

After a short time, I went out to see how he was doing and found him starting to drunkenly wander off into the woods, so I got him back and put him to bed. He woke up the next morning and didn't remember much of the previous night. He also never asked me for another beer. American beer is pretty light compared to ours anyway, and basically water when compared to my home brew.

One night there was a party next door and mom was visiting from Newfoundland. Feather was at our place for the night and since he and I had never tried moonshine before we decided it would be a good idea that night to give it shot. After the party wound down, we decided to go for a ride on Feather's bike, a 750 Norton. The baffles were shot so we wheeled it down to the road before we fired it up. I was holding onto the seat strap and we started slowly so we didn't wake up Judy and mom.

He suddenly cracked it into second gear and all I remember was seeing taillights. I must have realized I was off the bike and tucked and rolled as best I could. When I stopped, I still had a hold of the seat. When I looked up, I saw him up ahead sitting on the side of the road, bike idling, not looking back. I walked up to him and drunkenly asked if he wanted his seat back.

He said later that he thought he killed me and was terrified to come back and check because he would have to face Judy and mom; never even mentioning the other consequences that would have resulted from my demise. Facing the two of them would have been a daunting task for sure.

We went back home, and he tried to patch me up and picked gravel out of various parts of my body as best he could. I was badly scraped up as well as sporting a few minor cuts. I guess we were making enough noise that mom came out to see what was going on. Once she saw the two drunken idiots were alive, she just turned around and went back to bed. Moonshine does make a good painkiller for picking out gravel, but it was long gone by the morning.

I was married but was still dodging bullets and would for a few more years.

As time went on, I became less of a party guy because of Jennifer and did most of my drinking at home. But that only meant that when I went away, I would really go on a tear and lose myself in the booze.

8 DARKEST BEFORE THE DAWN

As my drinking progressed it was making negative inroads more and more into our home life, but I somehow still managed to be active in sports. I was posted ATR (Any Trade Required) to VU 32 Squadron in Shearwater as a driver and played for the Base hockey team. We played in the senior hockey league and this was where I really learned how to play hockey. I played with some very good players and they taught me a lot.

I also played fastball for the Base as a catcher. I had no ship to hide out on anymore, but still found lots of drinking buddies at the Mess. The atmosphere was considerably different from what I had become accustomed to, but I managed.

We had by this time moved from our trailer into Lakefront Apartments, which were PMQ's (Private

Married Quarters - Military housing for couples and families) in Dartmouth. This was much closer to work for both of us, and now I was surrounded by navy personnel, which suited me rather well as there were lots of drinking buddies.

This was a short posting, as after about six to eight months I ended up posted to FDU (Fleet Diving Unit) Atlantic and worked as a Hull Technician (HT). This was more like it, as it was navy again and to be honest the Clearance Divers drank more heavily than regular sailors, so I fit in rather well. This allowed me to play hockey for Stadacona and we played against Shearwater, which turned out to be a lot of fun. It was like what I would imagine being traded in pro hockey must feel like.

I found I loved this HT trade because it was hands-on doing many different tasks. I tried to re-muster but was denied. There were three HT's working there: a Chief Petty Officer, a Petty Officer second class (P2) and a Master Seamen, and they all took the time to show me how to do all the different aspects of this wonderful trade. I was really angry that I wouldn't get the chance to transfer into the trade.

It was here when my drinking was starting to change, and I would convince Judy to go to her parents' place in the Valley on weekends so I could drink with my diver buddies. I started arguments with her and then would stay aboard HMCS Granby, (which was the old frigate HMCS Victoriaville renamed) for a few days and get blasted. I have always considered that my drinking changed when I went out west but in retrospect, I was becoming a mean drunk during this time.

Yet another timeline I've had to re-write because of the drinking. It must distort time much more profoundly than I ever expected.

There was a guy whose nickname was Tuffy who I hung out with a lot, and he was a character of the first magnitude. He tended to stutter when he was wasted and one night we were out, and he called his wife and asked her what was for supper and she said "shit".

Without batting an eye, he said "Well, j-j-just c-c-cook enough f-f-f-for you and the k-k-kid. I d-d-d-don't think I'll be home".

I was with him another time when his wife was trying to figure out what to get her sister who was in the hospital and looked like she would be there for a while. Tuffy said in his stuttering way, "If s-s-s-she is going to be th-th-th-there that fucking l-l-l-long, get her a c-c-c-cactus". Like I said, he was a character. Hearing these replies as he stuttered through them at that time were some of the funniest things I had ever heard. I don't think their marriage was a smooth one for some reason.

During one of these times when I was staying on board and drinking with the guys, we got a call that a bomb had been found on a street in Halifax. FDU was called for explosive ordnance disposal (EOD) so we all piled in a truck and went to look after the bomb. I don't think I was even on duty. We were all pretty drunk, so when we got there the Petty Officer in charge had the police move everyone much further away -- including the police. If they had gotten too close, they would have realized how drunk we all were, and it would have been trouble. The PO recognized it as a dud, but we carefully loaded it up in lots of padding and off we went, with me driving. We were more of a safety hazard than the suspected bomb was.

Judy was now working evenings at a clothing store in Mic Mac Mall and she got me to promise I wouldn't drink while looking after Jennifer. One evening she called home and didn't get an answer so called her friend in the apartment downstairs to go up and check on me. When she did, she found me out cold on the couch with Jennifer running around the apartment very upset. She asked her friend to take Jennifer to her apartment and when she got home, I was passed out and she couldn't wake me. She was so mad at me but what could I say? She was right. I would have been responsible if anything had happened to our daughter. Another bullet dodged, but also another wedge was driven into our relationship.

The Diving Unit was scheduled for an inspection from Admiral Boyle and he was surprised to see that a Weapons Surface trade was working as an HT. He asked me how I liked it and I told him I loved it and had tried to re-muster, but my request had been denied. After a few more questions, he said he would look into it, but I never expected anything to come out of it. A few weeks later my re-muster came through. I wrote Admiral Boyle thanking him very much for giving me this opportunity, and then celebrated by getting drunk, locking my keys in the car and smashing the rear side window trying to get in with a screwdriver. My buddy Kevin helped me put a piece of plexiglass in as a replacement for the window, and when I say "helped" me, I mean he put it in himself because I was hammered.

I was posted to CFB Esquimalt in Victoria BC for four plus months to begin training as an HT. After six years as Weapons Surface, I was getting the break of a lifetime and was going to make the best of it. I was in my element and really got into learning all the different aspects of this awesome trade. The trade training was in various types of welding, plumbing, carpentry/cabinet making, sheet metal, locksmithing, blacksmithing, pipe and plate working, ventilation and air conditioning, habitability which included flooring, insulation, furniture repair and various other maintenance trades that were ship related. I managed to place third for my course which, with everything that was going on, was amazing.

I was lonely at the time so I got a job as a bouncer at the Junior Ranks Mess Club 44 which meant I worked evenings keeping the peace, sort of, until closing time and then we would drink for an hour or so. I only had a couple of incidents while working there and managed to handle them fairly well.

I found a guy throwing up in the bathroom and when I asked him to leave, he took a drunken swing at me which I avoided. I got him in an armlock behind his back and was walking him out when he put both feet up on the wall. I gave him a quick knee in a sensitive spot, and we were moving again. The closer to the door we got the more he started to resist so I ended up using his body and unfortunately his face to open the door. Once outside he threatened to call the military police on me so I told him to wait and I would call them for him. He decided to leave. I called Judy a while later after drinking a bit and told her I'd had to throw a guy out. She said not to worry about it, that it was my job, but I then explained to her that I actually used him to open the door!

Another incident could have turned out very badly for me. The club manager asked me to go and ask a guy to leave because he was in the club in work dress past six in the evening. This sounded pretty innocent but when I asked the guy to leave, he stood up and took a karate stance -- rarely a good sign. I turned a bit sideways to protect what I thought was my best part and started talking. I told him he could probably clean my clock but would be barred from the club and then wouldn't have a place to drink right after work. Remember, I was pretty tough but not stupid. That got through to him and he left, much to my relief. I was told that this guy was known for doing a lot of damage to a lot people, and the manager had known this. I went to the manager and told him that if he ever set me up that way again, he and I would have a real problem. No more issues after that.

I would get up, hungover, and go to school; then at noon I'd go over to the mess and pound back four or five beer, then back to school; rinse and repeat. After a month or so of this I was having fine hand tremors in the morning which actually worked for me in my welding phase as my "fine" shaking helped me do really good welds. I don't know if you've ever seen the WKRP episode where Dr. Johnny Fever took a sobriety test from a cop and found that his reflexes got faster the more he drank? It was much like that. Anyway, I'd then pop over to the mess and drink a beer, go in and throw-up and pound a few more back, which settled my stomach so I could get some food down; rinse and repeat.

The guys I was hanging out with were there on their year-long course and had the lay of the land. I started smoking marijuana for the first time with the guys and found it was fun, but I would drink as well and would end up as a paranoid drunk, which was not so much fun. The other guys were into a lot of other drugs as well, but I was too nervous to try them and, to be honest, I was having enough trouble with weed and booze.

It probably was a good thing I didn't go down that

road because with my addictive nature I would have been gone. Shortly after I got back home, a few of the guys got busted and were kicked out for using drugs. I had dodged yet another bullet, but I didn't avoid suffering damage from that experience because any semblance of the "fun drunk" was now completely gone and I was now a much, much, meaner version of me.

One thing that happened when I got back from the West Coast in the fall of 1974 that broke my heart was when Judy and I went to Jennifer's nursery school to pick her up and she wouldn't come to me. She was about two and hadn't seen me for over four months, and just stood there and cried. I didn't know what to do, but after a while she let me hold her but man that was hard to deal with.

Upon my return, I was posted to HMCS Ottawa as a Hull Tech. On the Ottawa I quickly found guys who drank like I did, of course, and we sure did it up right. I don't know how I managed to avoid being charged on many occasions because I should have been. We had a great crew and got along well. We put a ball hockey team together and played a bunch of locals every Sunday morning at a school in Halifax followed by drinking at the Fleet Club.

I was tasked with the job of tiling the Captain's flats (hallway) and got hammered and made a royal mess of the job, getting black tile cement over everything. My Chief peeled me out because I was a Leading Seamen

(Corporal) and in charge of the project. I felt embarrassed to say the least, because I had very little memory of even doing the job and spent a lot of time cleaning up the mess and doing it right. If the Captain had seen it, I would have been in trouble for sure.

Another time while doing work in the half-deck paint locker, we discovered that the bulkhead (wall) didn't go all the way to the deck-head (ceiling). On the other side was the officers' spirit locker (booze storage) and so we got an ironing board and were able to slide it under cases of beer and slip them through the opening. The whole mess got pretty hammered on all the beer we managed to "borrow" from of the Officers Mess.

A scary incident that happened during my time on the Ottawa stood out, because I easily could have died. We were leaving Halifax at night with HMS Britannia the Royal Yacht as her escort to the Olympics in Montreal when our anchor pocket door broke loose. The weight of this door a ton more or less and it was swinging free and slamming with such force it could be heard through the whole ship. We had to maintain our speed to stay with the Britannia but had to open up an inspection plat to secure the door and when we did the ocean came in with tremendous force.

I tried to lean out and get a chain hooked on the door and in the dark could not tell where the door was. It could crush me if I miss timed the hook up and it was so rough that it was not possible. I relayed the information and the captain turned the ship out of the swell to give me a safer opportunity to hook up and I got it done. Leaning out into the dark with the ocean and the door as immanent treats was nerve racking for sure and you can bet, I had a few after that.

Aside from all that, I did learn a lot during that time and was becoming a better tradesman.

I went off to Stadacona for my Pay Level 4 training and managed to end up in first place for that course. At the end of the course, we had a party and I really couldn't tell you what happened or how long I was drunk. I was getting to the end of my rope and was starting to think everyone would be better off if I wasn't around. The end was in sight but what the end would look like I really couldn't say.

I was getting worse by the day and I was now drinking on duty which can be very dangerous. We were in Bermuda and I was sent to Daniel's Head as shore patrol and got hammered so bad that when it was time to go back to the ship, they had to search for me.

I had passed out under a tree. The guys helped me back aboard and covered for me.

I went to a hockey game between the Voyagers and Russia with a bunch of guys from the ship and we had whiskey in a wine skin with us. I sort of remember the start of the game but then...nothing. I think it was two days later when I found out who won the game.

Blackouts were a family tradition, after all, and I

recall dad telling me of one that scared him badly. During the war they were in New York getting ready to take a convoy across to England. Of course, while there they were taking advantage of their shore time and got in some serious drinking. He became aware that they were at sea and went up to the bridge and demanded to know who took the ship out of the harbour (as that was his job). He was told that he had in fact taken the wheel to steer the ship out of one of the busiest harbours in the world, where the whole city and harbour was under a blackout order (no lights allowed). This was a different kind of blackout but maybe not so different since his mind's lights were turned out as well. He had no memory of doing that and quietly went back to his bunk.

Even when we were home, I was staying aboard the ship more and more to drink, and would even go to fire exercises drunk out of my mind. I'd somehow get away with it, but I don't know how. My Chief pulled me aside one day and said that I needed to get a grip because he wouldn't hesitate to charge me if I kept up this behaviour.

It was like nothing felt right anymore, and I just wasn't happy about anything. I was avoiding Judy and wouldn't have much of anything to do with any other family members if I could avoid it. I was not getting my next course when I thought I should have and that was frustrating me. I can now see that it was just another excuse to drink. Basically, I was pissed off at the world and not much fun to be around.

I treated Judy horribly during this time. If I had been treated that way, I would have left. I had convinced her over the years that it was her fault that I drank like I did. Mental abuse is just as bad as physical abuse and I was certainly guilty of that. She was basically a single parent at that time and was working as the Executive Secretary for the boss of a huge company in Dartmouth, while looking after Jennifer (and me as well). She had a lot of stress to deal with. I now know the clock was ticking, and the bell was tolling for me, but I was oblivious and couldn't care less.

She literally saved my life one night during the winter when I had passed out in the car after driving home. When I didn't come home, she had started cleaning (which was her go-to activity while worrying about me and my whereabouts), and at about ten at night she needed the broom and realized she had left it in her car. She found me passed out in my car which was parked next to hers, and half-carried me inside. This was the dead of winter.

That was the last time she came to rescue my drunk ass.

A short while later I was so drunk that I soiled myself and woke up in an awful mess. Now there's a proud moment to share, but that was where I was at. Judy didn't help me get cleaned up and I was mad and embarrassed and had to clean up my own mess. She had stopped getting me up and into bed at night if I passed out in the living room, and I would wake up in a chair, on the floor, or wherever I had passed out.

Another incident around this time was something I don't remember but that Judy told me afterwards: apparently, one night, Judy woke up and heard water running and jumped out of bed to find me taking a leak in the closet, totally unaware of what I was doing. Things were not good and were only getting worse.

Another close call happened when I got drunk in Shannon Park after celebrating the fact that I got picked up to play in the Regionals for hockey. Apparently, when I tried to leave, I backed into a chip truck and the boys took my keys; I went back and continued to drink. I must have managed to talk my keys out of them later on and I ended up driving home in a full blackout. In the morning I heard on the radio about a hit-and-run involving a kid in the area where I would have been. I was so terrified I went out to find the car and see if there was any evidence that I hit somebody. There wasn't, thank God, and CSI would have been proud of my investigation. I knew then that if I had found evidence that I had hurt a child, I would never have come back from that.

How many of these bullets could I dodge before one got me?

How bad it was getting was demonstrated by the fact that when Judy told me she was going out with friends in the evening, she was actually going to

Alanon meetings. My reply was classic self-denial as I told her she should keep going, since she obviously had a problem. By this time, she was getting tired of my foolishness because I could go missing for days.

I was on one of my runs (drinking) for a couple of days and ended up at the Fleet Club with a few of the guys from the ship. I want to mention that this was all pieced together after the fact because I was in a total blackout and have very few memories of the next few weeks. I apparently called Judy and told her that my friend Mark was having marriage problems and I was trying to help him. Her reply to me was, "He isn't the only one, and don't bother coming home". And she hung up.

I must have passed out in the car in the dockyard parking lot and then woke up in the wee hours of the morning, freezing. It was October 25th. I went back onboard and slept until they shook me awake in order to get me up for cleaning stations which I somehow managed to get through. I was one sick puppy for sure, but we had a hockey game in Shannon Park that morning and no matter what was happening I wouldn't miss that. After the game, we all went to the Ship Victory Tavern, and it was there that my life changed forever.

9 SOBERING TIMES

The effects of any drastic change are never clear at the beginning.

The following memories, thoughts, and recollections are at best cloudy given the state I was in at the time and are what I have come to believe happened. I've had to rely on those closest to me at the time to help fill in the many blanks.

I remember going into the Ship Victory tavern that morning and having the waiter drop two draft down in front of me. I also remember having the thought "you've had enough" and getting up without touching them and walking out. I didn't know what was happening to me and I was very confused and terrified. I also vaguely remember calling the AA number in the phone book (no google back then) and then chickening out when they answered.

I guess I drove around for a while and then must have remembered that I had heard my Uncle Keith was in AA, so I went out to his place. When I got there, he was drinking with a couple of guys from his ship (how fortunate). He gave me a beer and God I remember feeling so sick. I went outside and sat on the steps, but when I tried to take a drink, I found I couldn't swallow it. What had always slid down my throat without thought now felt like a cotton ball going down.

My Aunt Bonnie came out to see what was going on and I guess I told her why I showed up; she packed me up and took me out of there. As I sit here writing this, I just realized this must have been in the late afternoon as they were both home at the time. Up until now I had pictured this as much earlier in the day. This is where my memories get very hazy because for the past forty years, I thought that she took me and dropped me off at my first AA meeting. However, a couple of years ago I mentioned that to her, and she said, "You don't remember, do you?" She then told me that she made me call the AA number again and that a member came and picked me up in the parking lot of the Penhorn Mall to take me to my first meeting.

I have absolutely no recollection of that event. This was a blackout of a different kind, and time was out of sync I suppose. Like I said before, sometimes the stories we tell ourselves become our truth.

I have a picture in my head of standing at the foot

of the steps of Club 24 on Queen St. in Dartmouth leading up to the meeting hall and thinking this is the end. I also remember thinking a bit later that Club "24" was a strange name for an AA group (not knowing it stood for twenty-four hours, not 24 beer). It felt like I was walking up to the gallows and I must have looked it too. The member who brought me to the meeting was an older guy and he got me coffee and quietly talked to me until the meeting started.

I sat through it all and don't remember much of it except at the end when they asked if I wanted to say anything. I said, "I'm Bob and I'm here to find out if I'm an alcoholic or not." One of the older members looked me in the eye and said, "Son, if you came through our door, you probably belong here". Deep down I guess I felt like I did. Of course, by this time I had worn my welcome out just about everywhere else anyway. I assume the member who picked me up drove me home and dropped me off but again, I have no clear memory of the event. I suppose AA was a natural place to seek help as I had known about it my whole life, and it was a lifeline that was at least familiar to some extent.

When I walked into the apartment, I do recall Aunt Bonnie who had been there chatting with Judy got up and walked out. Smart woman! I was left standing just inside the door with Judy sitting on the other side of the living-room on the couch. I looked at her and clearly remember dropping to my knees and bawling like a baby. That moment is burned into my brain because I finally saw in her eyes the damage I had caused and felt the pain I was responsible for. I believe that was the moment when I truly surrendered and accepted the truth about who I had become.

Judy told me later that when Bonnie had come to see her, she asked if Judy knew where I was. Judy said at that moment she thought I was dead. She was very surprised that I had gone to AA but held herself in reserve as I had played games before.

I must have taken a week's leave as I was detoxing cold turkey at home and was in really bad shape. By the time I quit drinking, I was up to between 18 and 24 beer daily, and often a pint of rye. I would buy the pint "for Judy" who didn't even drink rye. The body and mind don't respond well to going off that much booze suddenly. It wasn't until fifteen years later that I found out how Judy managed during that time because I guess by then I had crawled inside myself and don't remember much, aside from some vague images of hallucinations which scared the crap out of me.

I read Eckhart Tolle's book The Power of Now recently and he describes coming out of the void, as he called it, with a feeling of peace and connection with everything. My experience was I would say somewhat different. Perhaps the "voids" we experienced were different because I was definitely not at peace with anything and felt separated from everything. My journey was a slow process and it would take years in some areas to gain that feeling of peace. I read early on that Bill W, the co-founder of AA, had a similar experience to Tolle's, and this always left me feeling short-changed. We all follow our own path to arrive at where we want to be, and all paths are relevant in the end.

Withdrawal from alcohol is very dangerous and should only be done under the supervision of medical professionals. The fact that I came out the other side without serious repercussions was more by good luck than anything else. I think that's why my memory of that time is so poor, and the fog lasted for months. I had no idea how dangerous alcohol withdrawal could be and also didn't know a damn thing about PAWS (Post-Acute Withdrawal Syndrome).

The people in my AA group were fantastic and literally started the procedure of putting me back together as a human being. The horrible thing is that I have no memory of the people from that group. I know I had a sponsor, but I couldn't tell you who he was as the details just won't come to mind. It was probably one of the older guys but, hell, they were all older than me. I have met two people who were around during that time, but I can't say I remember them (or them, me) but I was sailing during this time as well and was away a lot.

I had very few coherent memories for the next couple of weeks. I know I went to AA meetings because I later followed their directions to get to a meeting in Boston when the ship docked there. I was twenty-six years old at the time but much younger than that mentally, probably around seventeen or eighteen maturity-wise, if that.

I know there were a few other younger members in the local groups, because we would travel to meetings together. I still had a license, though I really don't know how, and I would pick them up and drop them off. We had a meeting on the way to the meeting and another on the way home. I think we were clinging to each other for dear life and even with that level of desperate camaraderie I still couldn't tell you one of their names. It's a lot like a movie where you can recall the soundtrack but can't see the picture, so you remember things happening but can't describe the scenes.

There was a young woman who was the daughter of an AA friend of dad's who was in the NS Hospital who I started driving to meetings along with the others. Because we were young and our interests differed from the older members in all but recovery, we decided to start a young people's group with the guidance of some older members. After a short while we decided to have a dance and Judy came with me.

After the dance, Judy asked me who the blond girl was. When I told her, she asked if she was the one I had been driving to meetings. When I said yes, she said, "Not anymore you're not!" I guess she noticed her watching us all evening and got a bad vibe from that. My mother had forewarned her that the women in AA could be dangerous, because they could share at a level the (sober) wives couldn't. I was oblivious to all of this and saw no harm in taking her to meetings, but I wasn't about to go against Judy's feelings at this fragile point in our relationship.

It's funny, but I warn people of that attraction now to help them avoid those very same pitfalls. The old timers always used to say, "underneath every skirt there is a slip". Not very politically correct these days, but then neither is a relapse.

This just brought back a story mom told me which I feel illustrates how much she struggled in those early days of dad's recovery, and even before. Her frustration before dad sobered up manifested in acting out in the only way she could. When dad came home and passed out, she would beat on him to relieve her stress and frustration knowing he would wake up and not remember why he was sore and bruised. Not highly recommended but later I would get to understand her thought process.

Before the AA dance, Judy and I had gone to a dance at the Timberlea Legion with one of my shipmates and his wife. This was the first time I had danced sober and it was an out-of-body experience. I clearly remember how awkward I was and felt everyone noticed my awkwardness. I didn't trust my shipmates and I got Judy to taste all my pop (soda) drinks to make sure no one had spiked them. It was just the beginning of a long list of firsts which we all live through in that first year of sobriety. Of course, as everyone got drunker, my anxiety increased because I had made the mistake of traveling with them. I never made that mistake again and made sure we always traveled on our own so at least I had an exit strategy.

I had been sober a little over a week and had just physically detoxed when I had to go back aboard ship as we were sailing to Boston. Judy took me to the ship that morning and I know we were both scared of this trip. To say I was fragile would have been a gross understatement. I was almost late getting onboard as we both were prolonging what we felt was the inevitable.

All I had with me was my AA Big Book and the Twelve and Twelve (Steps, and Traditions), and some suggestions from my group. I recall I asked what I could do to fill my time while at sea as drinking had been my only pastime and I had few other interests at that time. They asked me what I enjoyed as hobbies and I couldn't come up with anything other than drinking. They asked what I liked as a kid, and all I could think of was drawing and building things. They told me to focus on that.

I was always a prolific reader and started reading the Big Book and Twelve and Twelve. I found I could relate to a lot of the stories in the back of the book and the explanation of the steps and traditions started to make sense to me. I also started to draw again. I still have some of those first drawings, which I drew on Bristol board in charcoal and then glued onto wood. I found that the drawings smeared when I varnished them, so I went to drawing right on the wood, first with pencil and then with fine markers. I also made a lot of spoon racks. This turned into a great way to make extra money, as well as to fill in many hours of down time.

We finally arrived in Boston and I did exactly what I was told to do when we docked. As soon as we had a shoreline (telephone) I called the AA number and was told where a meeting was that evening. They gave me the address that was just across the Boston Commons and I made my way there that evening. That meeting came close to knocking me off my wagon as it totally overwhelmed me. Dad always said being on the wagon was just transportation to your next drunk; you either drink or you don't.

Our meetings at home might have a dozen or so members. When I walked into this meeting, it was in a huge room with what felt like hundreds of people but might have been just under a hundred. Still, it was too much for me and I was getting ready to bolt when an old timer recognized the look and started talking to me. He quietly spent the meeting talking to me. What he said I couldn't tell you, but I remember feeling that he genuinely cared. I knew I couldn't go to meetings there as they were just too big and intimidating. For those who know me now this must sound like someone else but for me at the time everything was intimidating and brand new.

So now what?

How was I supposed to survive Boston if I couldn't go to meetings? I couldn't go ashore with my drinking buddies and really didn't know anyone else who didn't drink like I used to. We are advised not to go ashore in a foreign port by ourselves but staying aboard where everyone was drinking in the mess wasn't a viable option either, so I needed to come up with a plan.

I took the lesser of two bad choices and went ashore alone. For the first time in my many visits, I finally got to see some of Boston. I walked along some of the route that Paul Revere was reputed to have travelled. I went to the USO and got tickets to the Russian Circus, which was a very cool experience. I also went to my first museum. This all helped me stay sober and sane but the biggest help with that was when I found out there was a betting pool on board ship as to how long I would last before I started drinking again. Now, I realize you don't know me, but once I get angry, I'm a hard guy to sway. As a result, I really owe whoever started that pool a debt of gratitude.

I arrived back home sober and, to be honest, I don't know who was more surprised, Judy or me.

"Here's Johnny!" comes to mind from the

Shinning, as I'm now starting to realize what an insane all-time, first-class asshole I'd been over the past few years. This getting in touch with the reality of where addiction has taken you is gut-wrenching to say the least, but necessary.

One night shortly after I got back, I asked Judy a question I was really scared to ask: "Where do we go from here?" I was terrified of the answer and couldn't believe my good fortune when the reply finally came. She simply said, "Let's just see where it goes and take it a day at a time". I never asked that question again, because even after all this time I don't want to give her the chance to change her mind.

Over the next several months I went to a lot of meetings when I was home. When I sailed, I now knew a few guys I could safely go ashore with, so things slowly started getting better on that front. I was attending so many meetings back then that after a few months Judy said she wasn't seeing me any more than she did when I was drinking. She asked me to cut back on the number of meetings I was going to. I struggled over that request for a couple of days and then finally had to tell her that I wasn't strong enough yet to cut back on the meetings. That was very hard to do, but my recovery had to be put first or nothing would work out.

I recently heard an analogy that sums up hitting bottom and what surrender means and it goes like this. When one gets to a point where their choice is to live or die, they have officially hit their bottom and have to surrender. They may surrender to the fact that can't stop and will carry on their addiction to the ultimate end. If they surrender to the fact that they have chosen to live they have to give up their power and submit to change. When someone surrenders in a war, they lay down their rifle, sit down, put their hands up, and wait to be told what to. When I heard this, it described exactly what I did in my early recovery. Once I surrendered, I had no desire to pick up my rifle again and followed directions without question, even though some of those directions were very difficult to follow.

After a few months, Judy shared with me that the week I decided to sober up she had actually found an apartment for her and Jennifer and had been talking to a lawyer. That was really hard to hear but I totally understood where she was coming from. She was responsible for our daughter's safety and she deserved a much better life than I was capable of providing for her at that time.

I believe now that my Higher Power had a lot to do with the timing of my decision to stop drinking. Now, early in my recovery I was having a huge struggle with the whole concept of a Higher Power and it would be a while before I was able to realize any of the impact it had over my life during this period of my recovery.

I wasn't sober all that long when it was suggested that I speak at an open meeting at the NS Hospital.

Reluctantly, I said I would. I've heard it said that the fear of speaking in public is stronger than the fear of death; that people would rather die than get up in front of a crowd. When we got there to put the meeting on, there was a huge crowd and I was scared shitless. I spoke anyway, because it was a suggestion from our group and at that point, I didn't feel like I was in a position to negotiate anything they asked me to do. They knew much better than I did what I needed at that time, so I trusted that.

I felt like I stumbled through it but afterward someone came up and said they got a lot out of my talk. I found this personally hilarious as I couldn't tell you what came out of my mouth, but maybe it was just the fact that I was six months sober. Perhaps that may have helped them, because there was very little recovery for me to speak of at that time.

In the fall of 1975 and the early part of 76 Judy and I were both working but I usually had a part-time job as well. I'd sling beer when I was still drinking, which meant I basically made no money as I drank up everything I earned. Once I had sobered up, I made and delivered pizza for a friend from the ship who had just bought a franchise, and so I actually managed to bring a little extra money in. We were both unhappy living in that apartment in Dartmouth and spent most of our spare time in Kentville at Judy's parents'. By that time Judy's mother Marion was starting to warm up to me a little bit.

I'm not sure how long this took but my timelines were pretty messed up. For years I have shared that it took two years to gain Judy's trust back. I remember her asking me each time I went out where I was going, who I was going to be with, and what time I would be home. She didn't trust me, and for good reason. I recall going out the door with my hockey gear one night and hearing her tell me to have a good time. It wasn't until going down the stairs at that old Lakefront apartment that it hit me that she hadn't asked the usual plethora of questions. I figured I had her trust once more, which was a huge step for me. The only trouble is, we moved from Lakefront in February of 1976 so that must have happened much earlier than I remembered.

One moment stands out quite vividly, from when I'd been sober for a few months. For some strange reason I had not been able to tell my father that I was now in AA. I had blown this encounter up in my mind because I thought dad would say something like "Oh, not you too!" or "That is just terrible!", but when I finally blurted it out on the phone and was waiting for what I had imagined he would say he floored me by saying, "It's about fucking time!". Of all the people I was hesitant to tell, he should not have been on that list at all. I don't really know why I was afraid to tell him, but my guess is that shame played a large role. He was overjoyed that I had found my way into the fellowship and really became a vital source of information on recovery after that.

Judy and I had to rearrange our social life drastically, which was hard because all our friends were partiers and we couldn't hang out with them safely. This was an awkward period and when we did go out, I was not a very comfortable human being. We avoided most of those social settings and relied on each other. This is not an easy thing for a young couple to do but the alternative was just not acceptable. When I became uncomfortable in a social setting, I would let Judy know and we would find a way to remove ourselves from the situation. We began to put all our efforts into our family and still do, to this day.

My first sober Christmas was spent at Judy's parents' place. Judy came up to me and told me that Frank (her father) - God Bless him - had told the family that there was to be no alcohol there over the holidays. I went to Frank and thanked him for caring so much. I knew he just wanted to help me, but I explained I would feel more centred out because everyone else would feel like they couldn't act normally because of me. I explained that if I became uncomfortable, I would go for a walk or a drive, or just play with Jennifer. He accepted that and the holidays passed without incident or awkwardness.

After Christmas, we decided to look for a house in Kentville. I was going to be sailing for the foreseeable future and that way Judy would have support when I was gone. In February of 1976 we bought a small three-bedroom bungalow on Camhill Court in Kentville, just across a large field from Judy's parents. I was getting to some meetings around Kentville but because I was sailing a lot, I never really connected with a home group there. That move helped look after the tension of too many meetings as well. We became pregnant again in April, and I finally got my Pay Level 5 course and was to be posted to CFB Esquimalt BC, for a year starting in June.

We are told in AA not to make any big decisions in the first year of sobriety and to take it easy. That shows you how well I follow directions, and with that experience early on is it any wonder that my AA connection was always off the normal path? Here I had just bought a house, moved to a new town, then moved to a different province, and was having a second baby. All of this happened during the first eight months of my sobriety.

My pathway is not necessarily a well-worn one, but somehow it worked out for me. I really do think it worked because I truly believed there was no other option. I still feel that way. I could drink again and lose everything, including my life, or not drink and have everything that means the world to me.

Now all I had to do was learn how to live again.

10 CROSS COUNTRY

In July 1976 we set out to drive across the country after renting our house in Kentville to another couple for the year we would be away. Jennifer was four by that time, and a good traveler. Thank God! It was a military move, so all of our expenses were covered, and they packed us up as well. All we had to do was get there.

We took eleven days to drive across the country. We stayed with my brother in Ontario for an extra day and did an extra day in Calgary where we ran into a fair number of "Maritimers" in the couple of days we were there. The Calgary Zoo was really something and we all enjoyed the animals, but more importantly we needed the break from driving. Judy was four-plus months pregnant, so there were a lot of bathroom breaks. For me this was hard because when I'm in "drive mode" I like to make as many miles as I can in a day. I now know in my advanced years that nature doesn't just call for bathroom breaks, when it comes to a pregnant woman, She screams.

After leaving Calgary, the drive through the Rockies was spectacular, to say the least, and I finally knew what real mountains actually looked like. We had never seen anything like them, and we were amazed at the sheer height and ruggedness. The rivers had a turquoise colour a bit like the Caribbean Sea, and the road wove alongside them most of the way through the passes. The Kootenay Valley was a beautiful drive. It was a very fertile area, a lot like home actually, but with real mountains and not the hills we call the North and South "mountains" in the Annapolis Valley where we now live! We drove straight through the City of Vancouver and caught the ferry across to Vancouver Island.

We got off the ferry and drove to Victoria, where we stayed at the Craigflower Motel in Victoria, and then got to work looking for an apartment. We were there for about two weeks, staying in a little housekeeping cottage with two bedrooms. The first morning there we were woken up by the shaking from a minor earthquake which we mistook for a big truck passing by the motel! I think it was a bad omen as the process of finding an apartment turned out to be a real hassle. Most apartments didn't want children, if you can wrap your head around that. Dogs and cats and probably any other kind of animal were fine... but no kids.

The apartment we ended up getting was close to the fleet school which was great for me as I could walk. We just barely managed to convince the superintendent (Mr. Fast) that we would not allow Jennifer to run wild in the building. It was funny because as wary of her as he was, within a couple of weeks she had Mr. Fast (who always reminded me of Mr. Furley on Three's Company) and his wife wrapped around her little finger.

Victoria is a beautiful city and is very British in mindset. They even serve high tea at the Empress Hotel. The population was heavy on young professionals and the old British guard. We always referred to it as "the land of the newly wed and the nearly dead". The grounds were immaculate and often surrounded by well-manicured hedges that gave it a very English feel. The local pub was called the Tudor House; anyway, you get the picture.

My course started and at orientation I noticed a section that was called "Ship's Stability". I asked what that entailed. The instructor said it was a combination of algebra, trigonometry, and physics, and I said you may as well post me back home because my math ability was basically non-existent. He told me that if I stayed with it, I would eventually get it and so I didn't turn around and flee but stayed to give it a shot. The rest of the course was trade related and I had no problem with any of it.

I did stick with it like he said, but after four of the six weeks of Ships' Stability I was still completely in the dark and getting more and more frustrated. I just couldn't make any sense out of it. I would spend all day at school trying to grasp it and then be up until midnight or later working at it. The light finally did come on and I was finally able to understand that by using applied math I would be able to figure out how the ship moved when weight was shifted (added or removed). For the first time, I could see that math was actually useful and once I saw and understood that fact, I no longer feared it. Later in my career I actually got quite good at it.

I ended up third on that course, which astonishes me to this day, given how chaotic the rest of my life was at that time. I tried the AA meetings while we were stationed out there, but I couldn't seem to fit in to the west coast vibe. I'm sure that was on me and not them. Without the benefit of the meetings, my strategy was to not allow any spare time to let thoughts of drinking encroach into my head. I see now that I used sports as an alternate addiction to get me through. I like to say an alcoholic is still an alcoholic even when they aren't drinking, and this is how I managed my obsessive, compulsive nature.

I played on the Base hockey team, the Base fastball team, the Base soccer team, the school hockey team, an Intermediate "A" hockey team, the school broomball team (I don't even like broomball) and helped them start up a floor hockey league. We had a new baby boy (Rob) in December, halfway through the course. Oh, and just for the hell of it I taught myself how to do macramé. We lugged those macramé plant hangers around for years.

So, if you think about it, the third-place finish for my course was outstanding!

Being busy may have been my way of coping with things but it's also a good method to get through life. To this day I have never been able to understand the concept of boredom. There is just so much to do in this world we inhabit.

We had my mother come out for the birth of our baby and that was the only family we saw for a year. I can still picture Judy walking across the hospital parking lot when her water broke. The look on her face was priceless. I was amazed when this little guy was born as we didn't know until the birth what we were having. Gender parties in those days came after the baby was born. I was pretty excited and actually got lost on the way home, the perfect mix of happy and exhausted. Judy was two weeks late so mom only got a few days with the new baby before she had to go home. We were a bit down after she left as we were once again on our own.

I honestly don't know how Judy put up with all my extracurricular activities and study time. She was the only one holding it all together as I continued to struggle with finding my way through growing up. Thankfully, we made it through that year without any major catastrophes and headed home. Other than a small two-hundred-mile detour, the trip went well, but more on that later.

The birth of my son was the highlight of living on the island. The scenery was also incredibly beautiful. One place that stands out as one of the most beautiful places I have ever seen on this earth was Butchart Gardens. My mom also got to see it, and she really loved it. It was built in and around an old quarry in order to hide the mess that was made, due to the removal of the ore.

We spent a long weekend at a campground on Lake Cowichan with Chuck and Elaine (friends we made from my course). I took Jennifer and Judy out for rides in the canoe and both of them really enjoyed that. One morning Chuck and I were fishing just as the sun was coming up and we saw a bald eagle dive down to the lake's surface and snag a big steelhead trout before snapping back upward and flying back into the sunlight. It is a vision I will never forget for its pure and natural beauty.

Judy was breastfeeding Rob at the time and unfortunately for her he had developed teeth very early on. This, coupled with how funny he found it when he'd bite her and she'd scream, made it a pretty rough process after a while. The doctor told her to yell at him when he did it in order to scare him with the hope that this would make him stop, but this didn't work very well at all. I can still hear Judy's scream echoing through the quiet Douglas Fir-shrouded campground at Lake Cowichan.

I can't remember if he stopped after that or not, but I also know he was introduced to the bottle around that time.

While we were out there, we visited a man who made burl tables and I bought a burl slab of Birdseye Maple that was three inches thick and about three feet long. I still have that piece of wood and have diligently carried it wherever we've gone since then. I've had that piece of wood since 1976 and have, I hope, finally found the base to make it into a coffee table which I will give to Rob, since it is from his birth province.

I got to play in the West Coast Regionals with the Base hockey team and got selected to wear an "A" for them (Alternate Captain, for anyone not into sports!). I also was able to play a fair amount of golf there as well and on some very beautiful courses. The golf happened more on later training courses, however, as I think if I had added four-hour rounds of playing golf to my year-long course and all the other activities it may have been the final straw for Judy.

We didn't get to travel much while we were in Victoria for that year as Rob was not good in the car. As a result, our plans of going south into the United States and along the coast highway ended up not happening for another twenty-five years. With all my training taking place in Esquimalt, I spent close to two years on and off on the West Coast, and for the most part enjoyed it.

When we got off the ferry in Vancouver on our way home, I wanted to stop and get a map, but Judy said we didn't need one. We came to a fork in the road (I think it was in Cache Creek) and ended up following the road less travelled; a great line I just came up with, tongue in *creek*... I mean cheek.

We drove for hours and were seeing less and less population, so we stopped at a place called the Hundred Mile House. I asked the guy how far it was to Kamloops and he said: "Well, you have to go back a hundred or so miles and then from Cache Creek it was just a couple of hours. By the time we got back to Cache Creek, we were beat, and the kids were very fussy, so we decided to stay there. As I said, Rob was not a great traveler and cried a lot, but we eventually made it home in around eight days.

You go faster on the way home. Especially with a crying baby in the car.

We got back to the East Coast and I had been posted to HMCS Annapolis and ended up sailing as soon as I got home. I only spent about six months on her because I got my promotion to Master Seaman, and there was already a Master Seaman there, so I was posted back to HMCS Assiniboine. During my time on the Annapolis we did an Arctic cruise which was amazing. It is a place so different from the rest of

Canada. We got to fish Arctic Char with the local Inuit, which for me was a dream come true, and we caught some really big fish which we cooked up and ate right out of the water. You can't beat that. The water was so pure and clear you could see the fish following your lures.

We were tasked to transport some village elders and families between the villages. These were incredibly friendly people and they took full advantage of the cheap prices in our canteen. We took the time to hike some of the most rugged, barren and beautiful country I have ever seen. I remember we climbed a large hill and when we looked back the ship looked like a toy sitting in the bay. Once we crossed over the crest, we were alone out on the land and it felt like we were the only human beings in existence. A very unique experience. We almost stranded the motor workboat while getting dropped off, because the tides up there drop incredibly fast. That was one of the most unique cruises I ever got to make while in the navy and it was in our own country.

We crossed over the Arctic Circle and so I was made a "shell back", I think it was called, by King Neptune's Court. This was a court made of guys who had either crossed the Arctic Circle or the Equator. They dressed up in the appropriate costumes and put us through a disgusting ceremony which consisted of being covered in all kinds of garbage mixed into a slurry. Once applied we took an oath and then were dunked in a Zodiac (boat) full of sea water which was straight from the Arctic Ocean and beyond cold. I have pictures of that somewhere. All in all, it was a lot of fun.

Once we got home, we got settled into our little house in Kentville. I think it was about a thousand square feet. It was a nice little house on a cul-de-sac, so it was safe for the kids to play, and the neighbours were great and watched the kids as well. Judy could walk across the field in a couple of minutes and visit her parents.

Jennifer started school in Port Williams in 1978 and Rob eventually had the run of the street. He had a little circuit set up on his bike where he could score cookies from the neighbours. In addition to my own sports I was also able to help another navy friend of mine coach a Midget baseball team in Kentville. We had a lot of fun with that, and the kids were great to work with; however, due to sailing I missed a lot of the season.

I also got to play hockey in Canning with Hatt's Wood Choppers in the suburban league when I wasn't sailing. This was a really fun league, and rough, which suited my game perfectly. There was one guy that I actually knocked out twice during the season with clean, hard, body checks. We played the old Olympic rules where you couldn't body check in the neutral zone and this guy would skate with his head down and didn't look up until he was over the blue line which was a pattern I picked up on pretty quick. I timed my check just as he crossed the line and caught him with his head down. Twice.

Some of those guys I still play hockey with today -- some forty years later.

I had a neighbour who had a fishing boat and I would go out and help him sometimes. He ran a tub trawl and I would cut bait and bait the hooks and set them in the tubs so they would run out when the anchor was thrown overboard. It required a very strong stomach to reach into a bait tub of fish covered in a disgusting slime and cut them up. You had to be careful when the hooks were released from the tub because if hooked it could take you overboard or rip you open. He had no winch, so we hauled each line which had over a hundred hooks on them, by hand. They were very hard to pull in! We caught a lot of dog fish, which look like miniature sharks, and a ton of skate both of which we threw back. We were after halibut and flounder and did manage to get some. That was hard work but fun and being on the water is always nice. Even peanut butter sandwiches tasted amazing out there.

I sporadically attended AA around the Valley but never hooked up with a home group as I was sailing so much. That is the excuse I used anyway. I think in retrospect that I had become somewhat of a loner by then. I totally believed in the program and had adopted the principles as the way I now lived but had grown used to being on my own. I don't know if that is good, or bad, but it is how I walked my journey. Like I have said, my journey did not follow the normal recovery path by a long shot.

I was now getting heavily into my self-study phase, which consisted of a lot of self-help type books and tapes. I remember even trying those subliminal tapes where there are positive messages hidden in wave and nature sounds or music which were designed to retrain the brain. I knew I had to keep working on myself in order to improve the person I was becoming. I had read a ton of recovery literature by this time and knew to filter the self-help stuff through that because I knew I was, and always would be, first and foremost an alcoholic.

In the spring of 1978, after getting back from three months down South with the ship, I hurt my back really bad and had to sleep on a backboard for two weeks or more. We were playing hockey in the fleet tournament and during the game I made a quick move and my back went out. I had to be carried off the ice and was driven to sickbay at Stadacona. I was on a gurney waiting for x-rays and in a lot of pain and they asked me to get off the gurney, but I couldn't bear any weight.

The pain was through the roof.

They did the x-rays and determined that there were no breaks that could be seen and said they would have to admit me for a week or so. Now, I had just returned home and would have none of that, so I refused to stay. Did I also mention I'm hopelessly stubborn? I told them I could sleep on a backboard at home and be with my family. They didn't like that but could see there was no give in me, so they finally wheeled me outside to wait for Judy.

When she got there, I was really cold from sitting outside for over an hour and in a massive amount pain. We managed to get me in the car and the drive home, which took another hour, and was pure torture. When we got to the house, Judy and a neighbour got me inside and tried to ease me into bed, but it was too painful, so I told them to just let me fall straight back onto the bed. So that is what they did and although it hurt like crazy it was better than the easing procedure (and much quicker).

All they sent me home with was Tylenol, which was just mean spirited as far as I'm concerned. I was on that board for the whole two weeks and maybe more and to the best of my memory I had no physiotherapy afterwards, mainly because I had given them such a hard time, I guess. My back has given me problems over the years and flares up now and then. I have to use a back support when doing any kind of sport or working where there is a lot of lifting, bending or twisting. If I'm on my feet for a long time, the brace helps.

When I got my medical records on retirement there is no mention of that injury which really sucks because

I can't prove the injury happened while working, and thus can't get a pension for it. I've tried to find anyone who remembers the incident but have had no luck, so no affidavit as proof is possible.

I went south in January of 1979 for three months and while I was away Judy had to live through our basement wall almost collapsing. There was an unusual thaw in February and water got trapped between the pavement and the frozen ground, giving it only one way to go. It burst through the basement wall and opened up a four-inch crack along the entire length where the water just poured in. This all happened a month before I got home but she didn't tell me, since she knew I couldn't have done anything anyway. The funny thing was that at the time Frank (her father) was in Moose Jaw visiting her sister Dianna so he wasn't even there to help. Her 16-year-old brother Steven brought a sump pump over but neither he nor Judy knew how to set it up. Eventually she contacted the engineer at Frank's work in Kentville and he arranged to have the wall shored up and she was able to clean up the worst of the mess. I'm sure Miss Casey our old case worker would have been proud of how strong she had become.

Jennifer couldn't wait to tell me all about it and blurted it all out as soon as she saw me when I walked off the ship. We had to wait until the warm weather arrived before tackling the repair. Our home insurance didn't cover it because they said it was "an act of

God". Judy had a "go bag" packed for her and the kids by the front door in the days after this happened because the house would make all kinds of sounds as everything re-froze. She was prepared for a fast exit if the wall decided to let go.

Judy worked with me in the spring moving dirt and cement blocks when we found out she was pregnant with Tracy. When Judy was pregnant, she was no shrinking violet. She was already a pro at hard labour (pun intended), so no worries. I had a 30' cement basement wall poured and then the final two courses I did with cement block. We also poured supports for the other wall and I made it look like a fireplace in the basement. I did a lot of work in that basement and made a pretty cool recreation room, which turned out really well and gave us more living space. It was a Tudor style and the roof looked like marble. I got this look by painting with high gloss white paint and while it was still wet lit a roll of tar paper and moved it all around and the smoke made lines and shadows that looked just like marble.

While we were living there, we used to go across the field to visit Judy's parents, which was so convenient. Then a local developer started to develop the land in the field by putting up apartments right up to our back line. So much for privacy and space. I had a nice-sized garden along the back line and let an older lady from the apartment building plant some things in it.

While we were there, we got another dog, which proved to be a problem for Judy as this animal would only listen to me and when I was at sea it caused a lot of problems for her. One night in a bad rainstorm, the dog got free and Judy had to chase him down in her nightdress. He would not come in and she got soaked but she finally captured him. The next morning, she called the dog catcher and had him relocated so when I got home the dog was gone. I'm only thankful that by this time I was pretty much house broken, and not causing any trouble, or I might have been relocated myself.

One day while travelling with a couple of navy friends coming home by way of Port Williams, a station wagon coming towards us much too fast didn't make the turn and flipped and rolled several times. It eventually came to a stop on its side. By the time we reached them, they were crawling out of the car, drunk out of their minds, and they were wondering how they were going to get to the Legion now.

Neither one of them had a scratch on them. Imagine that. One of them pulled out a cigarette and was looking for a light and my friend told him to wait until we got far enough away from the car before he lit up. He drunkenly asked why, and it was pointed out that he was standing in a pool of gas and would probably blow up if he lit that cigarette. We wanted to be far enough away to not get caught in the explosion. That finally got through to him and he put the smokes away and then the drunken pair hitched a ride to the Legion, and we all went on our way. Just another day on the road home.

We enjoyed our time in Kentville and being close to family during that time, which was a definite bonus, and it was such a nice little house. In 1980 I got posted to Fleet School at Stadacona. I did the drive for a while, but the distance traveled every day made for long days and I was too tired to do much by the time I got home. We decided it was time to move back to the city.

We sold the house and once again moved into PMQ's and back into the fold of the Navy. After living in the valley on and off for the past four years we were now in the city and surrounded by all things military, which seemed somehow a step backward to me. We were again living in an environment where we knew how to function, and even thrive, but I only connected to a small portion of that lifestyle. For me it was my family, work, and sports, and that about covered it. To be honest, it is pretty much the same today.

11 A FEW TOUGH YEARS

In 1983 I was posted to HMCS Huron, a Tribal-class destroyer, and this was a big step up from the DDH's (Destroyer Deck Helicopter) I was used to. I ended up being 2/IC (second in command) of the department and worked for Dave Monk, who was an awesome Chief. We had a great bunch of guys (about ten or so) who worked very hard for us. The ship was so much roomier and more comfortable than the old DDH's and much more modern in every way.

There was a tremendous amount to learn and I loved the challenge. For my trade we had to tackle every system on the ship (other than the electrical system) and the engines themselves. We had to trace all the piping systems and know where all the valves were located so we could isolate very quickly. It was the same for the air handling system, which we had to shut down during emergencies as well. Knowledge of all the spaces and what was surrounding them was required for damage control and repair.

It is really important to know what is on the other side of a bulkhead (wall) when you weld onto it or have to cut through it. It takes months just to trace and draw each system and commit them to memory because if a pipe is broken, or flooding or fire is in progress, there's really no time to look for a drawing.

It is good that all the ships are the same and once you learn one you learn them all, but each ship requires a walk-through to see what may be slightly different due to changes made over the years. When you are at sea, there is no one to call when the shit hits the fan, so you have to rely on everyone knowing what to do immediately.

We went on a NATO cruise and it was long but enjoyable. One event from the NATO trip that stood out for me was what I not so fondly called "funnel diving". What that meant was we had the acoustic sheeting in the funnel -- the chimney that exhausted all the heat and fumes from the gas turbines -- which was breaking up and pieces were fouling the flight deck with small pieces of metal. These metal pieces were dangerous to helicopters landing and taking off and could create an engine failure and cause a crash. This was picked up when they did a FOD (Foreign Object Damage) inspection which is carried out before and after each take-off and landing.

After finding this out, when we got into our first port, we rigged a tripod over the funnel opening and were lowered down on a bos'n's chair to pop rivet patches over the damaged acoustic sheeting. We had to wait until the engines cooled down before being dropped down that black hole, and it took a few hours each time. Even though the engines were off for hours there was a lot of residual heat in the funnel and it was hot work. I can tell you it was hard to do because when you are sitting on a piece of wood suspended by ropes (bos'ns chair) it is extremely difficult to gain the leverage necessary to pull the pop rivets tight. I'm sure you know how uncomfortable it is sitting on a wooden swing seat. Try working from one for a few hours.

We then had to check it in every port after that to ensure the patches were holding, and because I knew where to look, I had to be part of the inspection team. I never got ashore the first night in port, which is when I started calling it "funnel diving". I guess it is more like spelunking (cave diving) in reality. (That's for my daughter Tracy who called bullshit when I used the word "spelunking" and she had to look it up before she believed me).

This was another ship where I got more active in working the AA program because there was a need there. Like every ship I served on after starting my recovery, I made it known to the Executive Officer (XO) and the Doc that I would be available if they found they had someone who was struggling with addiction. I never thought that it would be one of my guys who started getting into trouble, but that's what happened. He was going ashore and causing trouble when he got drunk and it was starting to affect his work so a few AA members and myself started putting on meetings. He attended them and the XO sent a young officer to us as well. We carried the meetings on during the entire NATO trip and I know it helped me over that time. I'm not so sure about him.

We took the ship into refit in Port Weller, Ontario and I was tasked with putting all the books and work to be done during the refit in order. The main book was called the Kalamazoo, but I have no memory of why it was called that. It literally listed every piece of equipment that we were responsible for as well as its make-up and believe me when I tell you it was a massive document. That was a tremendous amount of work, but I really learned a lot from doing it.

We arrived in dry dock and the work really began. We were set up in a hotel in St. Catherines (just a short drive from the dry dock) which is where I lived for the next four months or so. My normal workday would be ten or twelve hours, with many longer than that. It didn't matter since I would rather put time in there than sitting in that hotel room. It is amazing how the longer you stay in a hotel room the smaller it gets. I can't imagine what a prison cell would be like year after year.

I was able to take my motorcycle onboard when we

went up for the re-fit, so I had transportation while up there at least. I made a rack to carry my golf clubs and got to play some very nice courses around the golden horseshoe region. I played with a few guys from the ship whenever I got the chance and it was up there that I finally broke into the seventies for the first time. I was missing the family more while there than at sea because we were on land and in the same country. It was just different.

About halfway through the refit, Judy was able to come up for two weeks. My Chief and the Chief Engineer gave me the whole two weeks off because of all the overtime I had worked to that point. This was the honeymoon we had never had (only thirteen years after the fact). We did the tourist thing and really enjoyed our time together. The best part was that it was on the government dollar. I'm such a romantic.

We did Niagara Falls so many times we got tired of seeing it. There is a lot to see in southern Ontario and we saw as much as we could fit in. It was a wonderful but brief time for both of us and we would really need it to help carry us through the tough times ahead.

I had met a lock master and he invited us for a tour to see how the locks worked to raise and lower ships in order to transit the canal, which was really cool. The big Laker boats had only inches to spare on each side when they came in the lock, and to see these massive ships raised or lowered depending on which way they were going was an amazing sight. He showed us the gears which controlled the water flow and they were huge, but a lot of the work was done by gravity which is truly ingenious.

Two things happened during that refit time that stand out for very different reasons.

One incident that happened was when one of the workers fell in the hold and was injured badly when he landed headfirst on the steel framework. I was onboard and heard the emergency announcement and was one of the first to arrive. The man had fallen off the staging onto the steel frames and was unconscious and bleeding badly from the head. I organized the duty watch emergency team while tending to his head wound and doing a preliminary assessment of his condition.

We determined that we had to get him off the ship and to the hospital ASAP. We got him strapped in a stretcher and fortunately there was a large hole cut out of the ship's side which we got him through. The dangerous part was that the hole was around thirty feet above the dry dock floor. The crane operator lowered a large bucket and we carefully put the stretcher on the rails of the bucket and me and the Dry-docks safety officer got in with him.

We were in the air halfway to the top of the dock when he came to and tried to get up. He was a big guy and very disoriented which was a bad combination because we were somewhere around sixty plus feet in the air by this time. We got him calmed enough to get us safely on the ground and the crane operator lowered us so softly we hardly felt the touch-down. He was taken to hospital and thankfully recovered from his injuries. I ended up with a Bravo Zulu accommodation from the Admiral for the quick action we took to help him.

I had complete trust in the crane operator after that incident and when I had the chance to go up in the bucket to take pictures, I took it. I'm pretty sure my fingerprints are still in the hook holding the bucket because at the top I was many feet over the masthead, and it was a long way to the ground; but I got some amazing shots.

The lock master I'd met was good friends with the twin brothers who owned the Niagara Falls Canucks, the Junior B team, and he got me and a couple of other guys a chance to skate with the team. We worked out with them while they were going through training camp and, when the season started, the coach asked me if I would be one of the trainers until the refit was done, so I got to travel with the team and be on the bench during the games.

What a great time that was to see how these great young, talented hockey players prepared and played this wonderful game. I have had the chance to be on the ice with some really talented players over the years, but this was the most fun and best learning experience I have had in the game. It really helped me when I ended up coaching high school hockey some years later.

It was during this posting that dad gave me about a three-acre piece of land in Kinsac. I was so excited that I would be able to build my own house, and I started to figure out what I wanted to build and decided on a log home. I began researching various types of log homes and settled on a cordwood style. Judy and I visited different cordwood homes in Nova Scotia and New Brunswick to get a sense of how they looked, and along the way met a few characters. I even went out and helped a guy work on his house, which helped me see the amount work that went into them.

I started out by clearing a roadway in and then the land, where the house and garage would sit, which was heavily forested. I did it mostly by myself. I bought an old one-ton dump truck to help with everything and as much as Judy hated it, it came in very handy. To get to the building site I had to cross a small brook and swampy stretch so to do that I sourced about a hundred old railway ties and made a corduroy road across the wet area. I loaded and unloaded the ties by hand myself and placed them before covering them with shale. I tried to move one recently and have no idea how I could actually have carried them. I was a lot younger, for sure, and in really good shape but god those things are heavy. The truth was I had very little money so most of the work was done on my own, but I did have some help from a few guys from the ship on occasion.

I found a stand of fire-killed spruce out on the 103 Highway toward Chester and made a deal to cut what I needed for a really great price. I lost a couple of weeks because I cut my knee with my chainsaw, but not too badly. They didn't stitch it because a chainsaw makes a pretty wide and messy cut and just used tape to draw it together instead. This fulfilled the prophesy of the salesman who sold the saw to me in the first place. His words after the sale were "Congratulations! You are now part of the club of those who have been or will be cut by a chainsaw." Thanks, buddy.

Otherwise the work was going quite well until we hit a major roadblock… actually, two.

The first was that the roadway into the land was a right-of-way from the old owner. I wanted a clear deed to the right-of-way and to get it I had to get all the family members of the deceased person to sign off on it. For whatever reason, I had to also show the deceased original owner had been given a Christian burial. I found his gravestone in a church cemetery and all the local family signed off on it. There was one family member who lived in Ontario and I figured I'd get that signature while the ship was in refit in Port Weller. But it was just a formality, or so I thought.

The second roadblock was a line dispute with the man who owned the adjacent property. It was over a small slice of the swamp area, if you can believe that. He was a county councillor who, I think, didn't want me building behind him and used his clout to cause me grief. He even had me dig up the culvert in my road and made me put in a highway grade one and cover the shale as it didn't comply with the bylaws on books. It is a good thing I had been sober for years by this time because I hate to think what I may have done to him in my drinking days.

The roadblocks did me in eventually as the one family member in Ontario was married to some union guy who thought I was trying to put something over on them. He wouldn't let his wife sign off so I had no clear title to the right-of-way but could still use it to access the property. I was determined to not give in to the neighbour - my stubborn gene, I suppose, but by now Judy had decided she was not going to move out there and live in the woods with the kids with me at sea so much. She wanted to know what she'd do in the winter and I told her she could get out no problem -- with the dump truck.

She hated that truck!

I eventually had the land sold to a couple who wanted to move a trailer on it and, when he was moving the trailer in, the neighbour told them about the dispute. I lost the sale and almost got sued over that. That confirmed to me that the neighbour just didn't want anyone behind him. They say the good die young, and he lived to be a hundred or more, so enough said.

The worst part is the only person I could sell the property to was, that neighbour and we ended up losing between fifteen and twenty thousand on the whole deal which was a huge setback for us. He was willing to trade my three acres for a building lot next to my brother but by then we were done with Kinsac. It had caused so many problems between Judy and me that I'm surprised we survived it.

I had worked my guts out for months only to have to walk away. I think I was saying the Serenity Prayer hourly during that time. When dealing with this man, I experienced an anger I hadn't felt before and if my brother Ted wasn't present at the worst of our meetings, I'm afraid I would have ended up in jail for assault. Like I mentioned earlier, Kinsac was not finished with me, but now we were done for sure.

We were a bit late finishing our refit and were pushing the window when they closed the St Lawrence Seaway for the winter. On our way back, we were held up as a tanker ship had hit one of the bridges and blocked the seaway. For a while it looked like we would be stranded in the seaway for the winter, but they cleared the blockage and we made it home in time for Christmas. I was never so glad to see Halifax Harbour in my life. Dave Monk wrote such a fantastic evaluation report that I got promoted to Petty Officer First Class shortly after that.

Dad and mom had separated after forty-two years of marriage and I took a truck over to Newfoundland and moved her back from Clarenville. I took Jennifer with me for company and she did pretty well on the ferry ride over. Once we got there, mom got a guy to help me load the truck but before that happened, I had to get a tire repaired on a weekend in a small town which was no mean feat I might add.

The two of us loaded the truck and we headed home. The crossing was a bit rough and Jen was a little afraid, and a bit sick, but we made it. We almost didn't make it through the Cape Breton Highlands as I almost lost control on a sharp turn on Smokey Mountain. The truck started to lean hard and was up on two wheels and thank God I had packed it tight, because if the load had shifted, we would have gone over the rail and I doubt if we would have survived.

Mom got diagnosed with lung cancer in early 1983 and was given nine months to live. I was just finishing a Military Effective Writing course and had gone to the doctor with mom when she got the diagnosis. I then had to go back and write the exam right from there. I somehow passed that exam but I'm not sure how, because my mind was very much messed up from the news. The doctor had said that if she could be around the grandchildren, it would help take her mind off what she was going through. We moved all three kids into one bedroom and put mom up in the other. When the kids came home from school, the first person they called to was Grammy, which she loved.

When she would get coughing because of the lung cancer, Rob (6 years old) would get her a tissue and rub her back until she got over it. Mom dealt with her condition with calmness and bravery, and really showed me how to live. She had met a friend while in the hospital and they hit it off; she talked to her a lot. As I'd come to understand, no one is as relatable as someone who is experiencing the same type of thing as you.

A fair number of her family kept their distance for whatever reason. I've noticed that's quite common in these situations and is just part of their journey. One of her brothers said to us one time that he couldn't understand how we would disrupt our family by having her move in with us. I was floored and told him we did because we wanted to spend time with her, and that the kids loved having her there.

How do you explain that to someone who couldn't understand it anyway?

She loved going out and enjoyed family outings more than anything. On the occasion of Judy's parent's wedding anniversary that November, we all went out to Mother Tuckers in Halifax to eat and she wanted to go too. At the time she was using oxygen some of the time and took a coughing fit while there. Judy's father was there, a smoker for years, and after he saw what she was going through he quit then and there. He is now ninety-eight and still going strong. I believe that was a gift from my mother to him.

Just before she passed, she asked if she could invite her friend to dinner at our place. I went and picked her friend up and we had a nice supper and they had a good visit. I really think she knew the end was near and was saying her goodbyes. She was the glue that held our family together, and when she passed the get-togethers with the whole family went with her.

Mom and dad had separated a few years before her death (after 42 years of marriage) and one of the few things that upset her over this time was that she was going to die before him. As hard as that time was, I am so grateful for the time we got to spend with her.

Dave Monk (my Chief) gave me time off from sailing as it was nearing the end, and I really appreciated that so much. Mom became unable to climb the stairs to the bathroom at our place and so went to stay with my brother Peter close, to the end. She seemed to rally for a bit, so I went to sea for a few days and when we got in the Padre was waiting for me and I knew it was not good news.

Mom had gone into the hospital the day before and was now in a coma. I went to the hospital and spent some time with her, just talking, and it was so hard and still is as I write this. Judy was saying that she may still be able to hear but my inability to get sound to come out past the lump in my throat was something that stays with me to this day. The rest of the family came and went, and when she passed it was just me in the room with her. I remember pulling the covers up so she wouldn't be cold and crying like the baby I was, hers.

She was just sixty-three years old and far too full of life to be gone. Mom always attended anything the kids were involved with, and I think of her often as I get to watch my grandkids in all their activities. I know she would have loved the little ones we are blessed with at present. I hope I have the strength and class she did when my time comes.

On a more positive note, we ended up living in Wallis Heights for about five years and during that time I got to play hockey for Stad during that time. This time for the "old-timers" (over 35). I also coached various levels of ringette which I enjoyed as Jennifer played for some of the teams. She was a terrific athlete in all the sports she tried. My recreation time was mainly at the rink and Tracy had the run of the canteen and they all knew her there.

Rob started his hockey there as well when he was around eight or so because until his friends started playing, he really didn't have much interest. Once he found the ice, though, he was a natural. Judy was active in the church but me not so much. My line at that time was that she could look after the religion and I would look after the sports.

I must have been a pleasure to live with, don't you think?

A posting came through and we were off again. I hate to think how I would have handled (or not handled) these years if I was still drinking. Working with addicted people for most of my adult life has allowed me to surmise through their experiences what that would have looked like, and I shudder to think about it. Through it all I never considered drinking for more than a few heart beats. Thanks to my recovery I was able to play it all out to the bitter end in my imagination, and knew it just wasn't an option.

12 THE END IS IN SIGHT

As soon as I got posted ashore, we started looking to move out of PMQ's. One reason was that Jennifer was starting to hang around a pretty rough crowd and we wanted to provide a somewhat more structured social environment for her. Another reason was we'd had enough of PMQ life. I had noticed that some guys would live in them until they retired and then had no idea how to live in the civilian world. We didn't want that for us.

By this time, we had somewhat gotten over the sting of the Kinsac land debacle and wanted to get out of the city. We looked around the valley and decided on a place in Hantsport a little over halfway between the city and valley. It was a really nice house on Maple Ave. A very nice street in a quiet little town. I traveled back and forth to work on my motorcycle and really didn't mind the commute as it was a really nice ride. I got involved in both coaching and playing sports in our new community and once we got settled, I could see us living there for a long time. It was one of my favourite houses that we have ever lived in and we were all very happy there.

By this time Judy was working for a court reporting business in Dartmouth and could work from home because I was able to pick up her transcripts and drop them off for her. I know it's hard to process but keep in mind that these were the days before the internet... I know... how did we survive?

Our youngest, Tracy, started school in Hantsport but didn't take to it very well in the beginning. Judy walked her to school the first day and by the time she'd dropped her off and made her way home, Tracy was already there, having bailed immediately. Despite the screaming and crying she had to turn her right around and walk her back again. Rob managed to fit in very well and had a good bunch of friends quickly.

As for our eldest, I remember Jennifer going down to the outdoor rink and the kids making fun of her for wearing boy's skates. Of course, as soon as she got on the ice and started skating circles around them, they stopped making fun and wanted her to play hockey with them. After that, she fit in well and played all the school and community sports and made some close friends who are still in her life today.

My father had decided to move home from

Newfoundland right around that point and as is our nature we had him move in with us until he could figure out where he would settle down. I'd made Judy an office in the basement so then went to work making a bedroom for dad. He drove Judy a little crazy because she hated it when someone would look over her shoulder while she was typing, which is something he would do often, as well as pace behind her.

He didn't stay very long (about a year) before he moved back closer to the city. He was contracting, refitting small fishing boats with a new coating for the holds and was driving around in an old Lada which I believe is Russian for "small tank". I don't think that's accurate, but it would make sense given the fact it sure drove like one.

He was seventy years old by then and still crawling around ships, so I guess I know where I get my work habits from. He was also a terrible driver by this time and the only way the kids could go with him was if I drove. They all still have memories of him coasting down hills in neutral to save on gas, so I guess I also know from where I get frugal habits.

The apple, indeed, does not fall far from the tree.

I had tried to get posted to the ARC (Alcohol Rehabilitation Course) program at Stad. This never happened because it is very difficult as a hard sea trade to get posted outside of your trade. That would have been awesome for me but was just not in the cards.

It was June of 1985 when I got posted to FMG

Atlantic, which was responsible for doing maintenance and fabricating things that were too big for the crew onboard the ships to tackle. We did heavy plate and pipe work, as well as carpentry projects for the fleet and even had a foundry where we did casting in brass and aluminum.

I worked on what they called the Outside Party for the first few months, which meant I went onboard the ships to assess and carry out work. That is when I worked a job for one of our submarines and after that experience, I swore I would never sail on one of those sewer tubes. I always said that if I'm going to drown, I want to start from the surface, not be already halfway down if something stupid happens -- like someone opening the wrong valve to flush the toilet.

One of the most interesting jobs we did was to bend large steel piping which we filled with dry sand, sealed up and heated with huge torches until it was red hot. We had to use chain falls to put enough force behind it to bend it to the shapes required. The sand also had to be very dry because if not you would virtually make a massive pipe bomb. The moisture would turn to steam and expand in a very confined space which created an incredible amount of pressure.

I also became a pretty decent aluminum welder at this point, and it is very tricky stuff to work with. All the machinery was heavy duty and we often would cut quarter-inch thick steel plates with large shears and then weld it to fabricate various items for the ships. I learned a lot there and enjoyed all the various tasks we did.

The Dockyard itself didn't like us working on the ships because they felt we were taking their jobs. At one point we were tasked to do staging jobs so that the dockyard workers could work on the boilers. The very next morning the staging supposedly collapsed (with no injuries) so we had to undergo an investigation which cleared us of any fault.

We figured the dockworkers had destroyed it to show we didn't know how to do that kind of work, but we didn't have any evidence. I knew it was solid and we checked it over carefully before turning it over but, despite all that, after that incident we did no more work where they would take over the job.

That was my first introduction to unions. It wouldn't be my last.

My favourite position there was when I was in charge of the carpentry shop. We did up wooden plaques by the dozens for each ship before they deployed which they would use for presentations in foreign ports. I made a bar top out of a single 2 inch-thick by 20- inches wide by 12-foot long piece of mahogany for one of the ships which I remember turned out beautifully.

I also received a letter of recommendation for a set of antique sailors cast in our foundry. I mounted them in a wooden case on black velvet that when opened displayed them as a framed set. It was presented to a

Japanese Admiral. After a while I lost count of the picture frames we built. We cut the glass and backing to fit the frames for diplomas, various pictures, and presentations. Not only did we build the items, but we also finished them in our spray booth as well.

It was literally a one-stop shop!

While working there we did up lots of favours for people (referred to as "rabbits") and were paid with favours in return, or the standard bottle of booze and/or cigarettes. These rabbits were done with the 10 percent of material which was always written off on all projects; we always had extra material, if we were careful enough doing the various work orders. It was common knowledge that this took place but every now and then someone would try to stop the practice. The chief of FMG came down one day and asked me what I was building. I paused and told him that if I answered his question, he may have to testify at the court martial. After a beat, he promptly turned and left the shop.

Not long after that, he came in and informed us that we were no longer allowed to do favours for anyone. I said, "No problem" and stopped doing them right then and there. However, a couple of weeks later he came in and asked me if I could build a particular item. After he described what he wanted, I said it was no problem and that I would do it as soon as I got the work order. He said there was no work order, so I said, "Look, Chief, we're either doing rabbits or we aren't...which is it?" After that we were soon back doing them as per normal.

I was supposed to be there for three years but only lasted a year and a half. I always wondered if it was something I said. Nevertheless, I got a great evaluation before I left.

I was able to coach Rob in novice hockey out of Windsor and we had a great time with that team. They went to Provincials, but I missed it due to joining my new ship. I also helped coach my daughter in ringette out of Canning and we ended up winning the Jr. Belles division at Provincials that year. I would get home from work, pick up Jennifer, and we'd turn around leave right away for that frigid old Canning rink. Jen would change in the car and we would just make it on time for practice... that's right, practice.

In addition to all the coaching, I also played hockey in Windsor in an old-timer's league and lob ball in Hantsport, while still being able to play some with Stadacona Old-timer's and participate in the Regionals.

Judy really liked it in Hantsport as well and was getting involved in the community, but that ended when the navy had other plans for us. I was at FMG and about halfway through the posting when I got posted to HMCS Algonquin, a francophone ship. This was a bit of a problem as I don't speak a lick of French. Perhaps I pissed off the FMG Chief more than I thought. Who knows?

I flew down and caught the ship in Boston and we sailed to Bermuda where I finished my turnover. I was now Chief of my own department but still a P1. We were on the first couple of weeks of a NATO and I was on a steep learning curve as the head of department. Gerry, the previous Chief, helped out a lot but I sure could have used a couple of extra weeks. My crew was a great bunch of guys and really worked their asses off.

It was very awkward being on a ship where all the pipes (announcements) were in French. Early on I had to rely on people to let me know what was being said so that I could react properly. I was getting some idea of what an immigrant must feel like when dropped into a new country and culture. The fact that I knew the class of ship well, and ship's routine being pretty much the same everywhere, helped me put together most of what was going on, but it could be very frustrating.

As time went on, I got a little tired of the whole ordeal and being more than a little stubborn, it got to the point that when I heard my name on a pipe I would just sit there and not react. When someone would ask me if I was going to answer I would say that if they wanted me badly enough, they would pipe me in English. Turns out that strategy didn't work out too well and after a while I accepted that I was just fighting a losing battle.

All in all, it was a good NATO cruise and I got to

visit some amazing places that I had not seen before. The Canary Islands were beautiful, and we even got as far as Bodo, Norway which is located above the Arctic Circle. We traveled into some fiords and saw glaciers coming right down to the water. It would be similar to an Alaskan cruise, I would imagine, and I was being paid to be on it.

In the Canary Islands we played on a golf course that was built along the rim of an extinct volcano with a farm at the bottom of the cauldron. The only way in or out was by helicopter, which we got to witness while we were there. I remember golfing a round with my friend Rick on that course, and he had been out drinking the night before and was not in very good shape.

There was a balcony that overlooked the ninth green and when we got to the green Rick dropped to his hands and knees and threw up in the sand trap. Some of the members were having drinks on the balcony and gave him a round of applause. He acknowledged them with a bow, and we moved on to the back nine with as much grace and dignity as we could muster.

We also visited Cardiff Wales, home of the world's second highest tides (next to ours in the Bay of Fundy) and what a beautiful old city it was, and with very friendly people. Cardiff Castle was (for me) next to Edinburgh Castle in Scotland as one of my favourites. While we were there, I went to the local arena and met the manager who showed me how they made their ice which, as it turned out, was very different than the way we do it here.

As we did the tour, we came up with the idea of a hockey game between our boys and their local team which already had about six Canadians playing on it. I explained that we had the hockey gear but no skates onboard and he was able to get me on the local radio station where we asked the public if they could supply skates. Boy did they ever! There were hundreds of pairs brought to the arena and we ended up getting to play.

The game was in the afternoon and there were over 500 people in the stands. They were a great and boisterous crowd, probably due to a few pints in the pub prior to the game. To make it even, they split up the pros so that the teams were better balanced, and we had an absolute ball beating each other around the ice. It wasn't a no-contact game by any stretch and in addition to a few nice checks I scored a sweet top-shelf goal. The arena manager invited me to his place for supper before we left, and I got to meet his family which I thought was really nice of him. All told it was an amazing place and one I would love to show Judy someday. It was one of the highlights of my military sports career.

We had a cool exercise at sea during that trip as well where we towed various targets and the air forces of the NATO countries did firing and bombing runs. It was an amazing exhibition of raw power which you really had to be there to see, hear, and fully experience. I have pictures but it just doesn't do it justice. One of the jets we saw as a small speck on the horizon just above the water (on the deck) and within a few seconds it went vertical over us and hit the afterburners, making us all hit the deck. I'm surprised there was any glass left in the bridge windows. It was awesome!

We had a British Physical Education Recreation Instructor (PERI) on board by the name of Nigel who I started working out with. By the time I got home I was about two hundred and ten pounds and in fantastic shape. It really paid off when we had our own version of an Olympic competition in one of the ports. We were docked for two weeks of repairs and had to do something! I took part in swimming and football and even tried cricket for the first and only time. I had my bicycle on board at that time and got to see some of the countryside of Norway, but not a lot due to the sheer size of the mountains.

One of the most uncomfortable situations I got into was when we were anchored off of France and celebrated St. John Baptiste Day. Everyone got pretty much hammered and I didn't sleep much that night because a lot can happen to a ship at anchor when there's so much equipment running and those looking after it are not necessarily at their best. There may have only been a couple dozen sober sailors onboard, which made for a very nervous night for us to say the least.

While we were there, Judy had to go in for an operation. The best I could do was call her by short wave radio. Again, how times have changed. It was very awkward because I knew a lot of people were listening in. The very act of speaking on those things is hard to get used to, because whenever you finish talking you have to say "over" so the other person knows to respond, and the shortwave operator knew to make the switch. No Face Time or Skype back then, my friends. It was old school but effective and I remember the nurses at the hospital where Judy was having the procedure thought it was pretty cool.

On our way back from that trip I was posted and promoted on the same day! Another big change that came with mixed emotions. It was a good news/bad news scenario. The good news was that I was now a Chief Petty Officer Second Class. The bad news... I was posted to TRUMP Detachment Davie in Lauzon, Quebec. It was hard enough for me to be posted to a francophone ship, but now they were doing this to my family as well.

The funny thing was that the day before my promotion, as a P1, I struggled to get any respect as the head of a department and just a day later as a C2 I had no problems. Such is the military way I suppose. That actually made me start questioning the reasoning for some of the decisions made by leadership. I could give them sound information as P1 and be ignored while the same advice after my promotion was considered solid. I figured that if that was how things were done it would mean that the reverse would also be true, and that bad information would be accepted as sound on little more than the basis of rank which made me wonder about the logic being used.

The Algonquin was the first ship going into a TRUMP (Tribal Class Update and Modernization Project) refit which basically meant tearing it apart and modernizing just about everything, a process that would take well over a year for each of the four DDH-280 Tribal-class destroyers. I had to first get the ship ready to go into the refit and fortunately for me Gerry had done a huge portion of the work. I still had to bring the Kalamazoo up to date (no small task), and do all the physical work, like stripping out all the unnecessary things before going to Lauzon. Once we had the ship in the dry dock, I walked across the gangway and was then to become part of the TRUMP Detachment for the next four years.

Unless of course, plans changed. Which they always seem to do.

While I was getting the ship ready to go upriver, Judy was getting our house ready to sell. It was something neither of us wanted to do but we had no choice. I could have gone on my own but neither of us wanted that kind of long-term separation. She was able to get the house sold about three months later and I flew home to drive us all back to Quebec. This happened in December and, let me tell you, it was a pretty sad bunch that piled into the car leaving Hantsport.

I remember we had a crazy cat that would only let Tracy near her who gave us a real problem right off the bat. The cat hated the car and we had to drug it up (vet-approved medication of course) and put it in a cage in the back of the car. Jennifer was crying because she was leaving her boyfriend, Rob was crying because he was leaving his friends, Tracy was crying because everyone else was crying, and the cat was howling in its cage as we set off in our little red Ford station-wagon.

We made it about as far as Windsor (a ten-minute drive) when I pulled off the exit and dropped the cat off at Judy's brother's house with instructions to find it a new home. It may sound cruel, but it was far better than throwing it out on the side of the road! Tracy really had something to cry over now and the three of them were miserable for hours.

They pretty much cried until we got past Edmundston, N.B. which took over seven hours, and then they all wanted something to eat. I had to drive back into Edmundston, picked up some McDonald's and brought it back to the motel. They wouldn't eat any of it. When your kids want to punish you for something, they have a lot more tools at their disposal than you'd think.

We all arrived in Quebec City the next day and to my surprise everyone was still alive and on general speaking terms.

Our PMQ was not available by the time we got there so we stayed in a motel for about a week until it was finished. We finally settled into the PMQ in CFB Valcartier and, as it turned out, our next-door neighbour hated English people, so the welcome wagon definitely didn't show up to greet us. We had to share a driveway with them. Our PMQ was also right across the road from the school where Rob and Tracy went and the high school where Jennifer was to attend was only a little further away. These schools were on the base where there were about thirty English families. At recess time, they always kept the French students separate from the English students.

Jennifer already spoke pretty good French by then and fit in rather quickly. Of course, the fact that she excelled at sports made the transition far easier. Rob made friends easily and played Atom hockey which I helped to coach as well. I explained he wouldn't understand anything in his first practice and that he should just put himself last in line so that he could follow all the drills.

At the end he came up to me and said that despite not speaking French at all there was one thing he did understand. When I asked what it was, he looked at me with a smile and said, "The whistle". He was a comedian even then. Tracy really struggled for the first few months and Judy had to be in the window every day so Tracy could see her when she was out for recess. Eventually things settled down for her as well... eventually!

Judy really tried to make a go of it despite her inability to speak the language. She decided to take a French course with the government and made an appointment to go into Quebec City to register for the course. When she arrived, she told the receptionist her name and that she was early for the appointment but didn't mind waiting. Shortly after that a man came out and called for "Mrs. Early" a few times before Judy realized they were calling her. The interviewer then explained that the waiting list to take the French course was very long so that idea got shot down in a hurry. She eventually took a French course on the base which helped, but it wasn't as intense.

I remember we even had issues when we went to the bank on the base to set up our accounts. They would only speak to us in French and to this day we don't know exactly what services we ended up getting with them. The ATM was all in French as well which took a while to figure out. I remember asking strangers in line behind us how to access it. I also remember going into that same bank a few days after opening our accounts only to find the teller who had only spoken French to us was speaking perfect English to another teller. My optimistic outlook was being stretched to the limit.

This was right around the time of Bill 101, which stated it was against the law to speak anything other than French to customers, but that was only supposed to be at first. The government had spotters out, so retailers had to take it very seriously. It became quite obvious that the general attitude was that it was fine to make people suffer to prove a point and that really got under our skin.

Judy was determined that she would make them speak English when we went for her driver's license but despite her best efforts, we ended up leaving in complete failure. We eventually had to get a friend of mine to come with us to help us through the procedure. These were government offices in a supposedly bilingual province! While the rest of Canada tries to be bilingual, Quebec was at that time completely unilingual, right down to the road signs.

We found some odd things about living there that really stuck out.

When grocery shopping, all the isles were one-way only and God forbid if you ever went the wrong way. People would never give way to someone else if you made the mistake of walking the wrong way. Judy was shopping one day at The Bay and an employee was pushing a rack of clothes down an aisle toward her, so she stepped aside to let her pass. The woman stopped when she got by and said to Judy, "You're not from around here, are you?" I guess she was used to navigating with difficulty around customers who never moved out of the way.

Even when we tried to speak French, we were made to feel awkward. We stopped for ice cream once and I tried to order four chocolate ice creams and was looked at like I was from another planet. I asked him again but was met with the same result; a shrug and a blank look so we left again, entirely defeated. At least I was able to get along okay at work due to the fact that we worked in English, but Judy was struggling big time and the kids were really missing home.

Then I began to struggle at work as well, but for much different reasons.

The Detachment Commander (DC) and I had vastly different ideas about work, family, and extracurricular life. While I was involved in coaching, playing sports and doing things with the family, he was focused only on work. I remember him telling me once that I should not allow extracurricular activities to interfere with my work. My reply to him was, "Sir, there is life outside of work". From that point on, he was out to get me, a fact I didn't base on any mere feeling but from the mouth of another officer who I got along well with. After getting that tip, I went immediately into CYA (cover your ass) mode and kept a detailed logbook, along with my work log, to keep track of everything I did right down to a T. I still have that book today.

One fun thing I remember from that time was when I ended up going with the Valcartier Old Timers to play in the National tournament in, of all places, Cornwallis, Nova Scotia. The bus ride down and back was a bit on the lonely side, as I was the only Anglophone on the team, so I brought a Walkman and headset and a few good books that got me through that ordeal. We had a really good team and ended up finishing in second place, losing a close game in the finals.

I remember walking into the dressing room with the team for the first time in my navy uniform and all the talking stopped. I looked at everyone and said: "I'm an English protestant sailor who doesn't speak French worth a damn so don't give me a hard time and we'll get along fine." How is that for an icebreaker? I did get along fine and they were a good bunch of guys who all spoke English fairly well.

I made friends with our goalie and he invited us to his place for supper one night. His wife spoke no English and didn't seem too enthused about her husband having to translate the whole night, which made for an uncomfortable evening. At the end of the night while we were getting ready to leave, he turned to his wife and said, "So have you had enough English for the night?" He had no idea how that made us feel but it pretty much sums up our time in that province. By the time we left, we had had enough French for our lifetime.

Judy's parents and aunt came up for a visit in June and when their time was done, we turned around and went home with them for vacation of our own. It was really good to be home. I'd been in Quebec for about nine months at that point and near the end of our vacation Judy and I were on our way into Halifax when she turned to me all of a sudden and said, "I don't know about you but me and the kids aren't going back". That's the one thing about my lovely wife, she doesn't mince words.

I ended up going back to Quebec by myself and told them that there was a bit of a problem and that my family was not coming back. Judy had been seeing a specialist for her jaw pain in Nova Scotia before we went to Quebec and there was only one other place (Toronto) that provided the same treatment, so I was able to apply for a compassionate posting back home. The DC who disliked me went into full-on hate mode and made my life a living hell from that point on.

I managed to find a francophone Chief who wanted to come up, but the DC shot it down. He ended up giving an ultimatum to another Chief, who wanted no part of the posting, telling him that he either accept the posting or get out. I felt bad about that one because in the end he chose to get out. With just that one incident, the DC ended up being the cause of two Chiefs leaving the navy as once I got back home, I started looking for other opportunities as well.

Before plans to return home could be implemented, I had to spend several weeks in the PMQ with our dog, Lady. I felt bad because she had to stay home alone all day while I was at work. I ended up bringing her back to Nova Scotia with me. Unlike the cat, we made it okay, even though she wasn't a very good traveler either.

Judy and the kids were staying with her parents while she looked for a place to live. I drove straight through from Quebec to Kentville on a Friday night, and then back to Quebec on the Sunday in order to clean the PMQ and move into transition quarters (which was basically a room in barracks). I remember being given a hard time when I requested to come in late so I could exchange my linen. A young lieutenant who was apparently an understudy to the DC in the art of becoming an asshole was responsible for that and other little incidents that made the rest my time there as miserable as possible.

On my posting evaluation, they conspired to write up a horrible picture of my time there and asked me to sign it. I refused and they said that they would charge me if I didn't. I told them to go ahead. The fact was that my last evaluation detailed that I was outstanding in my role and that if they chose to charge me their careers would suffer, not mine. I also mentioned that I had a detailed documentation of all the incidents during my time there, along with witnesses who would back up everything. They backed down and rewrote the evaluation in a somewhat better light, but it was far from outstanding.

These were the people who finally gave me the

push I needed to leave the military, so I guess a belated and begrudging "thank you" is in order.

I knew that I would pay dearly for the compassionate posting because that was the navy way. I figured I would also likely end up with bosses very similar to them again, which was not something I was looking forward to, but I wasn't quite ready to leave just yet. In late November of 1988 I started work at the Naval Engineering Unit (NEU) Atlantic and was now responsible for any modifications proposed for the fleet. It was my job to investigate them to see if they were reasonable, and then check to see that they were done according to standards.

I enjoyed the work and got to visit most of the ships and the men I'd gotten to know over the years, but in the back of my mind I knew that my compassionate posting would come back to haunt me. I started to look at my options and ended up getting my GED grade 12 and became a Certified Engineering Technician which was available to me due to my service time and training. We rented a small house in north Kentville on Gracie Drive.

I began putting out resumes to any industry I could think of, without any interest coming back. By that time, Judy was working at the hospital and one day she said there was an opening in Addiction Services in the Detox unit, so I applied there but again got no reply. I tried again a few months later when another position was posted and again received no reply. When the third job posting came up, I remember saying, "Why bother?" but Judy coaxed me to apply so I did. I sent my resume again with a very short cover letter consisting of just one sentence. "If you feel I don't have the qualifications or I am not suitable for this work, would you please reply so I won't waste your time further, and you won't waste mine."

I got an interview.

I went into the interview, which was conducted by the charge nurse, Gail Wilson, who I later referred to as Sergeant Major Wilson (with respect). I had what I thought was a good interview and got a call a few hours later saying that I had the job if I wanted it. I believe I paused about ten seconds and then asked, "When do I start?". She asked how long before I could be clear of the navy and I told her a couple of weeks which worked out well for her.

I called Judy and told her we were out of the navy. Despite all the hassles we'd endured over the years, Judy panicked a bit because there was a lot of security in the forces. I also was going from forty-five grand a year to twenty-six, and even with my pension was still making about ten or twelve thousand dollars less than I had been in the navy.

Despite all that, I can honestly say that the decision just felt right in my gut.

I had about four months of leave coming to me in order to help with the transition; however, I'd be completely released a month or more before my six-month trial period was over. No pressure, right? I was excited for the new endeavour and began what was to be the next chapter in my life. Now I would be able to use all the things I'd learned in my many days of recovery to help those starting out on that same, long, difficult road.

13 DETOX

I can honestly say the next several years were the best education I have ever experienced. By the time I began working in addictions, I had been sober for fourteen years, and thought I knew a lot about recovery. I quickly realized how little I actually knew. My new beginning, however, at first was more of a reality check than anything else. I had moved from being in charge of highly trained men and top-notch equipment to making beds, cleaning up puke, and even giving baths.

Of course, I was a Hull technician in the Navy, and another name for us was "turd herders" (from unplugging toilets). Perhaps this was a foreshadowing of what was to come? Thankfully, because of that, messes in general gave me no real problem and that meant that I was more than qualified for the new adventure. Right.

I was also used to very little privacy, so that wasn't a big deal either. But these were very different messes and privacy issues, because the patients themselves were often embarrassed -- something I felt very keenly. It was awkward at times, but I managed to detach from that and make them feel somewhat comfortable.

Another learning curve for both me and Judy was that I had gone from being away a lot to now being home all the time, and even working in the same building! We had lunch together on a daily basis. After twenty-one years of coming and going it was a big change but, like everything else we did, we took it in stride and it actually worked out well.

I had also moved from a male-dominated environment to one that was mainly female dominated but was comforted by Gayle's military "no-nonsense" approach to work. She was a hard taskmaster but was pretty fair and I knew she cared deeply for the patients. But it was from my fellow counsellors and, of course, the patients that I learned the most.

When I started there, the counsellors began to educate me in what working in the field entailed. Like I said, I thought I knew a lot about the recovery process, but I really didn't. I had gained enough smarts in my recovery to keep what I thought I knew to myself and focused more on listening and learning. I spent the next six months amazed at what I didn't know, and what I had to learn to become somewhat helpful to the people who desperately needed it.

The information that was available for us to use for the patients was just as important for me as it was for them. I loved the tapes by Father Martin and Ernie Larson and still do, to this day. There were others that were very informative, but the presenters were not as impactful as my favourites. I gained a lot more insight from sitting in group and discussing these tapes with the patients and other counsellors. I slowly began to add my experience to the mix, and at the end of the first year I felt fairly competent.

I really have to give a lot of thanks to all the people who were a part of my early education. Everyone who worked there did so because they really cared and because, like me most were in recovery themselves. This allows for a much easier connection to patients. People can usually tell when someone is speaking from experience, because the words just ring truer.

Shortly after I started working there, I went home and told Judy about this guy who had showed up at Detox with nothing but the clothes on his back. We went right out and bought underwear, sweatpants and toiletries for him. When I brought them in to him, Gayle told me not to do that anymore as there was a room full of second-hand clothes that were used for that purpose. We both just saw a need, so we filled it. I would also take my barber stuff in and would cut hair when needed.

I don't think I've mentioned that I taught myself to cut hair when I was on the Huron and by doing that over a NATO trip paid for a two-week vacation to PEI. I got to be a decent barber but then again, I had a captive audience while at sea. Cutting hair on a ship at sea is not an easy task as everything is in motion and it takes a steady hand. I practiced on my son Rob first before the trip, and he did eventually speak to me again. I think being away for five months helped that process as well as the fact that the difference between a bad haircut and a good one is about three weeks.

Right around this time Judy and I decided to buy another house and found one on Oakdene Avenue in Kentville, which was a short walk to work. We bought it with the idea of renting out the apartment in the basement but never got that far as it would have taken a lot of work and money to get it up to code. Spare cash was not easy to come by at that time. It was great for the kids as the park was right across the street and we spent some fun times there playing hockey on the pond and soccer on the field. I used to practice hitting golf balls just like I had done at the park in Hantsport. I think it was there when I welded up a hockey net for Rob at Judy's parents' house, because her father Frank had a welder. I welded up some trailer frames for Frank as well, since he liked to build utility trailers.

We were short on money for Christmas that year, so I sold off my radial arm saw and some other tools to make up the shortfall. It was fine because Frank had a whole workshop I could use if I needed to build anything. I did some renovations around the place, but it just wasn't working out financially, so we sold it and rented a house out on Mitchel Avenue in Kentville. This was a nice house on a quiet, dead end street and I started catching the bus to work as we only had one car and my shift work was all over the place while Judy worked straight days.

I always maintained a very upbeat attitude at work, and this got me more than my fair share of time off, especially if my boss was in a bad mood. I learned that when her ears were red, her patience was short, and her mood was less than optimal. I'd be having a great time laughing and carrying on and she would ask me if my work was done. It usually was so she would let me go home. I think this was as much to get rid of me as anything else, but whatever the reason it worked out well for me.

Manipulation runs close to the surface in all of us, and I only just now just realized that is what I was doing at the time. I now know how slow some of my awareness takes, as that took place in the early nineties and I just recognized it for what it was as I wrote this.

I had one of our regular patients ask me if I ever got down and when I said, "absolutely" and he said, "bullshit", because he claimed he had never seen me down. I asked him if he had ever seen me whistling as I worked, and he said that he had. I explained that when I was feeling down, I would whistle something upbeat and keep my head up and work faster until I felt better. I don't know where that came from, but it does work better than letting the down feelings grow stronger by giving in to them and being quiet and moping around.

When I first started working at Detox, it was located in the old Sanatorium which used to be the TB hospital until that disease was virtually eradicated. The building was now used for Addictions, Mental Health, and Administration. They were in the process of building the Valley Regional Hospital on the Sanatorium grounds right behind us. We had our own cafeteria and the patients went down to eat there as well. It was a very small close-knit building and really had a homey feel to it.

I was still pretty green in working with sick people and made a few mistakes along the way. One incident stands out in particular and it showed how sensitive and fragile people are when they come in. There was a young woman who was scheduled for an x-ray but got up late. When she was ready, I took her down to the X-Ray Department and the other patients were sitting there waiting so I jokingly said she should just sit here with the rest of the old drunks and she burst into tears.

I didn't know what to do so I left her there to wait and went back upstairs with the incident eating me up inside. As soon as she got back on the floor, I went to her and apologized for being so insensitive. She let me off the hook by saying that what I'd said wasn't what made her cry but that she had been thinking about something else at the time. Maybe yes, maybe no, but I learned to be more considerate in what I said and how I talked to these very sick and fragile people.

I think this is what made me realize that addicted people are actually hyper-sensitive and that this is part of our problem in the first place. It's also usually what ends up making us seek self-medication as we are trying to avoid the emotional pain.

There was an older gentleman who once slept under the pine trees outside the building in order to make sure he'd get in first thing in the morning. It was a cold night in the late fall (if my memory serves me) when I saw him, and he was so sick that once he was admitted he was in bed for a couple days before he could even get up on his own. I was worried he wouldn't survive.

I was talking to a heroin addict and he was telling me how bad his addiction was and how much he suffered during his detox. I looked over and the old gentleman was trying to pour and drink a coffee. His shakes were so bad he spilled most of it before he even got it to his mouth. I pointed this out to the heroin addict to illustrate how everyone suffers when detoxing. It is known that alcoholics can die from physically detoxing from booze, but it is rare for that to happen from other drugs. Overdosing is usually the way people die from other drugs.

The best part of this story is that the old gentleman never took another drink after that detox which had been his twenty-something time going through this. I don't know what he heard or what changed but he ended up helping a lot of people in their recovery for several years and as far as I know he passed away sober. He had snow white hair and the big red nose commonly associated with life-long alcoholics, but when he walked into a room he actually glowed with gratitude and was always smiling. He taught me to never give up on people because you never know when the miracle will happen.

People would show up at our door often in the worst overall shape in their lives, but an equally difficult challenge came from the fact that after they were physically detoxed, they would most likely have to walk out and back into the same situation they'd just left. Without making any changes, most of these people were set up to fail and if they got lucky would make their way back to us. The change can't just be physical but has to encompass all aspects of their lives. To be honest, few are ready to make that commitment at first.

Once people start feeling better physically, they often forget how bad it was and only remember the fun times. Some would come with the idea that we would fix them with little effort from themselves which just isn't the case. Others would come because they were forced to in some way, but it doesn't matter how you arrive; it only matters how you leave.

My boss was very observant. She pulled me aside one day and told me straight to my face that I wasn't a counsellor. This took me off guard as that's exactly what I'd been doing for over a year, so I asked her what she was talking about. She then told me that while I was a very solution-focused person who could see what others needed to do, the patients wouldn't listen to what I had to say. I listened to what she had to say but didn't really understand it until a while later.

One day I was having a one-on-one session with a patient and saw for myself that despite the fact I could clearly see what he needed to do in order to get better, he was entirely tuning me out. I remember slamming my fist on the table and telling him that I'd like to punch him right between the eyes so he would sit up and listen to what I knew would help him. I don't have to tell you that this wasn't an approved counselling technique, and the look on his face told me very clearly that he would never listen to anything I had to say again.

I finally understood what my boss was trying to tell me earlier. No one cares how much you know until they know how much you care. That became my new way of dealing with patients from then on. I would catch myself telling them what to do and would just stop talking. After a pause I would ask them what they thought and would then just shut up and listen. After they talked for a while, they often would find their own solution and my job became much easier.

That was undoubtedly the best lesson I learned in my first few years working in Detox.

Counselling 101 is (1) Listen to the client, (2) Relate to them and (3) ask them what they intend to do about it.

I was also now back to having a home AA group in Berwick. I enjoyed the group and was working with a few people sharing what I gained over the years. I did that for a couple of years and traveled around to the various other groups in the Valley, which allowed me to get to know a lot of the recovering community. Working in Detox and going to meetings was a good fit for me and very helpful. I celebrated my fifteen-year AA birthday there, which I think was the last one I celebrated until my twenty-fifth.

Judy even baked a birthday cake for that meeting. Unfortunately, she lit the candles a bit early while she waited on the sidelines for me to finish talking and by the time, she brought it out, the candles had heated the icing which began sliding off the cake. She was embarrassed and swore she would never do another cake and was true to her word. It wasn't much of a problem as it was ten years until the next birthday anyway!

I don't know why I never celebrated my AA birthdays. I guess I missed so many in my sailing days that I failed to think about them much. For me it was just another day. Of course, I understood that celebrating these milestones helped a lot of other people by showing that long-term sobriety is possible, but for me it just never felt right due to the fact I wasn't overly active in the program for a lot of my recovery.

We would do sessions in our group room, and at that time everyone was allowed to smoke which was hard on most of the counsellors, who didn't smoke. When we moved into the new hospital, they were going to let that practice continue but we said we wouldn't do that anymore because it was bad for our health. My boss didn't like that much. I remember when we wanted to do twelve-hour shifts, she tried to stop us from doing that as well. She wasn't one for change. The Twelve Step sign that hung on the wall was literally brown due to all the smoking over the years and I figured our lungs were going to look like that as well.

Boy how times have changed!

It was around my second or third year in Detox that I was introduced to Amway. I saw it as a way to make up the shortfall in my salary from leaving the Navy. I was mostly captivated with the books and tapes available in the business, which were focused on helping improve yourself and taught how to deal with people, and I took advantage of it all. Judy was not thrilled with this venture and made it known. She looked at it as a cult and only took part in meetings or gatherings if I pressured her into it, which wasn't very often. I was not very good at it as I am a lousy salesman.

Judy didn't like the fact that you had to deceive people in order to get in front of them and explain the Amway concept. I saw it as a way to help people, while helping us, and sat down with people in recovery with the thought that it could help them as well. I approached some who weren't that strong in their recovery yet and that was not a smart thing to do. I don't think it led anyone to drink again but it took them away from what they should have been working on, something for which I still feel sorry today. I worked very hard at it and managed some modest success but could never seem to make a go of it.

After a while, Judy and the kids had an intervention with me, which I really needed but at the time resented. They sat me down and asked what I thought I was accomplishing. I told them I was trying to make things better for my family. But it was the next question that hammered the point home when they asked if I thought I was even part of the family. They never saw me anymore, and on reflection they were right. For about two years I would do a shift at Detox, go home, eat, change into a suit and be gone until late at night. To be honest, I was probably spending more money than I was making so I packed it in. I had to admit that my obsessive nature had taken me down a rabbit hole.

One night, coming home one night from Halifax after an Amway meeting, I was pulled over for speeding. I had to be at work for eleven-thirty and was flying. When he asked me where I was going in such a hurry, I said I was going to Detox. He did a double take. I explained I was working there and was late for my shift, so he let me off with a warning to slow down and then followed me for several miles to ensure I did. The look on his face, though, was priceless.

I'm almost positive that was the first time he had heard that line: speeding to get to detox.

I did attend most of the Amway rallies/conferences and even went to Charlotte, North Carolina to a big one where I saw a lot of successful people who had done exactly what I was trying to do; I could see that it was possible. That's where I saw Florence Littaurer and Zig Ziglar, two people I really got a lot of insight from and whose teachings I have used when working with recovering people ever since.

I did gain a lot of helpful information through the books and tapes in Amway and did have a spiritual awakening which led me back to church and helped in what I was doing at work. By the time I was done with Amway, I had drifted away from AA once again but was working with addicts, full time; this kept me well connected to my recovery.

Now that I was home all the time, I got involved coaching my daughter in her last year of high school in soccer and softball. We had really good teams and won the Provincials that year in Cape Breton for soccer, which was kind of full circle as I had also won soccer Provincials in Cape Breton about twenty-five years earlier.

We won Districts and Regionals in softball and hosted Provincials, if my memory serves me, but didn't win that one. I really wonder sometimes how I managed to get involved with so many different things, but it hasn't really changed much through the years. My boss said to me one time that I'd better be careful because I was burning the candle at both ends. My reply to her was, "Gayle, wouldn't it suck if at the end of our life we had candle left over?"

God I was cocky.

I was playing old-timer's hockey for Coldbrook with a bunch of really good guys as well as getting back into golf and was starting to have some fun again.

I'll share a story about my boss, because it shows the kind of person she was under all the gruffness. My cousin Vinney was killed by his son in a hunting accident and of course the family was devastated. I asked Gayle if I could leave early to go to his funeral in the Rawdon Hills and she said, "No problem". As I was walking out the door, she gave me an envelope with two hundred dollars in it for the family. She didn't even know them but felt that she should help out and asked me not to say anything about it. I'm only doing so now because she passed away some time ago and I feel it deserves to be noted. It really illustrated the old saying "don't judge a book by its cover". That was certainly true of her.

She left work one day and never came back.

She had retired and no one even knew. She hadn't mentioned it to a soul. It was the end of an era in Addiction Services, that's for sure. I think I worked there a year or more after Gayle left and Joan stepped in to take over the unit. I think that moving into the new hospital had created too many changes in how things were done, and it was time for her to move on. Joan had worked with Gayle for years, so the transfer was pretty seamless. My extra time off pretty much ceased, however, which is as it should have been after all.

Things changed a lot after we moved into the new hospital. The biggest change was that we didn't have a nurse in the unit all the time but had ready access with a call. We were looking after the patients on our own through the evenings and nights which was more stressful for us, to be sure. The nurses would come over to give medication and would drop in during their shift to see how things were going, but otherwise we were on our own. We had a couple of incidents with seizures that got a little on the crazy side, but thankfully we didn't lose anyone.

The years I spent in Detox were an amazing learning experience and I worked with great counsellors for the entire time there. I owe a great debt to all the people I worked with and learned from during the time I spent there. But as is my nature, I am always looking to move into new experiences so when they posted a position for the Evening Counsellor on the 28-Day Day Program, I applied and was fortunate to get selected. I walked back across the parking lot to the old Sanatorium (Miller Building), and into another fantastic learning experience.

14 THE 28 DAY PROGRAM

After six years of working in Detox, they posted a
position for the Evening Counsellor on the 28-Day
Program. I applied and got the position. Just as when
I started in Detox, I had an over-inflated opinion of
my knowledge about addiction and recovery. You'd
think I would have learned from my first experience,
but sometimes it takes thick Scottish skulls a few times
to fully grasp these things.

Once again, I kept my head down and spent the
next six months or so getting an education from the
people I worked with. This was a whole new level of
recovery and went much deeper into the inner
mechanics of working on oneself and trying to
implement lasting change for the better.

George and Brian were the daytime counsellors,
and between them had a lot of knowledge in guiding

people through these changes. I sat through all of the sessions in order to gain insight into what the clients were going through. They were no longer referred to as patients, but as "clients" and the important difference was in the fact that they had been sober for a minimum of six months (with the odd exception) before being admitted to the program.

After I got a sense of what the program entailed, I could easily understand why the clients became so upset from what was dredged up during their daytime sessions. They were uncovering a lot about themselves during the day that people don't always like to feel, so once the evening shift came around, I was kept pretty busy dealing with the daytime fallout.

I also saw a few areas where I could add some of my own experiences, gained throughout my years in the program as well as from my life experience. I had always been open to any information that enhanced my life and now saw that it could also help the clients.

One of the things I picked up from Amway was the breakdown of personalities, as taught by Florence Littaurer. It helped the clients gain a better understanding -- first of themselves, and second of other people, and why we behave as we do. The plus side to this was that it was a lot of fun, and the clients loved it as it enabled them to see people in a different light. They now began to understand that everyone is acting according to their own personalities, not necessarily in direct conflict with theirs, and that this was usually the root cause of the conflict between them. From my experience it seems that we are oftentimes attracted to the differences between us at first, but then set out to change each other to be more like ourselves. Strange.

There is a demonstration which I think clarifies this. If we look at our hands like two different people, with the tips of our fingers representing our strengths and the valleys between as our weaknesses, then when we clasp our hands together, we see that our strengths cover the others' weaknesses and we are able to bond together. However, once we are together for a while, we then begin to work at changing each other to be more like ourselves. Once this happens, our strengths begin to line up; we're no longer even trying to bond and begin clashing and bouncing off of each other.

Another session I would do was one in which I would show them how they gained their view of the world and how much more positive input it would take to overcome any negative they'd experienced in their lives. This helped a lot; to understand that change was possible only if one was open to looking at things differently. This was also around the time I started using another of my favourite sayings: "If you want something you've never had, you'll have to do something you've never done". I wrote that saying on the whiteboard in the Miller Hall and no one touched it for over six months, which shows the power of a good idea.

Despite the fact that my role was now to actively try and help others on their road to recovery, that didn't mean the work on myself was complete, and while there I had a lot of powerful moments of insight. I remember sitting in on a session done by our spiritual counsellor on dealing with old trauma when I had one of the most enlightening experiences of my life.

I was not a counsellor in these sessions but rather saw myself as part of the group and participated fully. The group was doing an exercise where we sat quietly and went back to a time when we experienced a traumatic event. On this occasion I went back to when my grandfather gave me the beating of my life. He asked us to feel the emotions and the feelings we were going through during that experience and with my eyes closed and focusing as much as possible, it truly felt like I was going through it all over again. When we were deeply involved in reliving the event, he then asked us to try to consider what was going on with the other person at that same moment.

It was not like a lightbulb going on gently. It was like it exploded in the darkness and for the first time in my life I understood my grandfather and what probably happened.

By the time the beating happened, my grandfather had suffered through something like four or five strokes and was trapped in a body that wasn't working very well. His right hand was drawn into a fist from all the painting he had done in his younger days and had no feeling in it at all. That was the hand he'd wailed on me with. I think the smart-mouth youngster giving a hard time to the person who had been looking after him for years, coupled with the fact he felt trapped in the wreck of a body, culminated in him snapping.

It didn't make it right, but it did make it understandable and I was able to forgive him. That was an awakening, for me, to the fact that there is always another side to what happens to us and that we tend to only look at the situation through our point of view. All I know is that I felt a peace of mind over that event that I had never felt before. Eric (our spiritual counsellor) did a few different sessions that I used to sit in on, and I can honestly say I always found them to be invaluable.

One of my favourite sessions was when he would do was a guided meditation where he took the group on journey up a mountain. When we got to the top, we met a person sitting by a campfire. The person had a sack and we were instructed to reach inside and take something out, which would have meaning to only us. I remember one of the clients received a golden ball and when asked afterwards what she thought it meant, she replied that maybe if she believed in God this is what she thought God might look like.

Everyone had their own gifts, and an idea of what each object meant to them. It was an interesting exercise that everyone seemed to enjoy. Later that evening the client who got the golden ball had a visitor who brought her a gift. When she opened it, there was an angel holding a golden ball. Now, you can make what you want from that, or just chalk it up to coincidence. I'm only sharing what I witnessed. But the woman in question took it as a sign to possibly rethink her atheism.

On my trip up the mountain, I ended up with no gift, which I thought strange and asked Eric about it. He, of course, asked me what I thought it meant and, after a bit, I said that maybe it meant that I didn't need anything, and Eric thought that was a possibility. I was, in retrospect, in a good place in my life.

Working during the evenings allowed me to interact in a much less formal setting than the day staff, and I was able to see the struggles the clients were dealing with as they worked through their issues. I would spend time with them as they struggled through their stuff and would then pass it on to either George or Brian in the morning so they could address anything that needed to be dealt with.

There was a custom that bothered me and that was on the night before a client graduated, the other clients would play a practical joke on them. This caused a lot of trouble at times as not everyone has the same idea of what is funny. I remember one practical joke ruining a pair of very expensive boots which turned a very positive aspect of the program into a very negative experience. Obviously, that's not the goal so

I thought something should be done about it.

I had read something in Chicken Soup for the Soul that I thought would be a better thing to do for someone leaving than a practical joke. I put together some short readings, poems and stories that were uplifting and inspirational and then got the other clients to write a short note to the leaving client with something they liked about that person or perhaps a quality they admired, along with their contact information if they wanted. I then put all of it together into a package for them and it became part of their graduation ceremony.

I really got a lot out of working on the 28-Day Program, but a steady diet of evenings for almost two years began wearing thin. It was about this time that Brian retired, and Reg moved into the 28-Day Program in his place. That left the Community Health Worker position open, so I applied and got it.

This was a totally different kind of position but the eight years I had spent working in the other two positions helped prepare me tremendously for this. This position turned out to be my favourite job of all, because it allowed me to spread the word of what addiction is, and that there is treatment and hope. It also included working with the recovering community in setting up and maintaining the Aftercare Program. I also had a client load of up to 70 people, and often saw between five and seven people a day. That is a lot of work, when you factor in the session notes for each.

This was by far the most demanding job thus far, but I loved it.

I was now out in the community doing presentations in schools and for any other group who was interested. I traveled around and put on training courses for anyone in recovery who wanted to become a contact person for the Aftercare Program. This would be someone with whom the clients who were leaving the 28-Day Program on completion could partner. Contact people are what made the 28-Day Program so successful, because there was someone waiting to work with the client until they had settled into recovery and obtained a sponsor. The school presentations were always my favourite thing to do, because I have always loved working with young people.

I was once asked to meet with a group of kids in middle school to see if I could help them change direction. We met once a week and there would be about five on any given day that would attend. After a few sessions I could tell they were losing interest, so I decided to change it up. I asked them what they wanted to be when they grew up. One said a lawyer, another a teacher, someone else a doctor and so on but when I came to one young man, I could tell he wasn't into it. I asked him what he wanted to be, and his reply was "I don't know". I then asked him what he liked to do, and he said "nothing," so I asked what he did after school. His response: "I get on the bus".

"Well what do you do when you get home?" I asked. "Get off the bus" he said.

I told him I would come back to him later and he smirked and seemed relieved. My last student was a little hellion who liked to say things to try and shock me and, of course, her answer to the question was classic. She said, "I want to invent a condom that rings before it breaks". With a straight face I said, "Cool! So now that you all know what you want, let's take a look at what you will have to do to accomplish your goal."

I took each one and worked forward. For most of their goals they had to first finish middle school, then high school, then university. A few required postgraduate work etc., and I even calculated how many years it would take for each. For the condom bell ringer, I said she would need two degrees: one in engineering, and one in marketing but I told her she would likely be very rich if she could get it to work.

I then asked them that if they really wanted to achieve these goals, what was the one thing they could do today to ensure it happens? They all had a puzzled look, so I said, "It's simple. Stay in school today, put some effort into it and don't hook off; then get up and do it again tomorrow. After the amount of time we worked out for all of you, you will all get to be what you want to be."

Then I turned back to Mr. "I Don't Know" and said, "As for you, don't worry about any of that because none of this applies to you. You have gone as far as you will ever go because you've already arrived at your full potential. If you don't find something to strive for, this is it." I hope the exercise had an impact on one or all of them but with kids you just never know! I would love to know what happened to them, but I lost contact when the school year was done.

One of my other favourite insights came to me while speaking at a Family Seminar, when I compared the addicted person to a puppeteer who kept everyone, they were close to on very thin strings that they operated. The job of the people around that person was simply to cut the strings and make the addict responsible for themselves. Mostly, this involved a conscious decision to stop reacting to them and their drama.

I remember being asked where that analogy came from after the first time I used it, and I had to admit that it just popped into my head when I was talking. I've always said that I will get about three original ideas a year and that may have been one of them.

I suppose if there's one thing I have an ability to do, it's to make certain concepts accessible to just about anyone. I remember speaking at Acadia University to a group of sociology students once and found it more than a bit humorous that a guy with a GED was lecturing university students.

Life is a very funny mistress at times and you never know what might come next.

No matter where I spoke, there would always be

someone who would come up and talk afterwards about how addiction had affected them or ask questions to see what they could do to help a loved one currently struggling. This really helped me see how far- reaching addiction is and made me doubt the stats out there that claim a mere ten percent of the population has addiction issues.

That particular stat came from, I believe, the 1950's or '60's and refers to alcoholism only. My guess is they don't want to do a thorough study including all addictions because the number would be, I'm sure, astronomically high.

I don't always learn my lessons right away, and sometimes I have to bang my head against a few walls to drive a point home. Money was still a clear and present concern at this time, despite my new position, so once again I delved into the business world -- in addition to already working full time.

One business I got into was selling vitamins with Shaklee, and the other was with Jewelway selling (of course) jewelry. Both ventures met with results similar to my previous experiences, but it was not with the same intensity as with Amway so neither stirred up the same resentments as before. Salesmanship for me, as it turned out, was a lot like baseball. Three strikes and you're out. Not since those days have I attempted to be a salesman.

I really loved this time in my life, however, because it allowed me to coach again and I got the chance to coach Rob for his final year of high school hockey. Rob and two of his high school friends, Shawn and Barry, transferred to KCA from Horton when the latter dismantled their hockey program; I volunteered to coach and was lucky enough to get it.

For me this was the highlight of my hockey-coaching career. By this time all the parents knew that little Johnny wasn't going to the NHL, so they were much less in-your-face and really just enjoyed the games. Of course, all hockey parents are experts - I know this because I am one of them - but high school for the most part was just plain fun.

I had various meetings with all the parents, but one sticks out in particular. One of the parents told me there were grumblings about how I was mixing up the lines and had no set power play or penalty killing units. At the meeting I gave out paper and pens and asked them to write out their issues, unsigned, and I would address them.

I gathered them all and explained why I was doing things the way I was. I explained that I was new to the players and wanted to see who could work well with whom and that once I'd done this and had a look there would be an official power play and penalty killing unit. These would not be set in stone, however, and would maybe change as I got to know the players and their strengths. I explained that for me the regular season was really nothing more than a training camp to get us ready for Provincials.

I made up a bunch of inspirational signs which I would put up in the dressing room before each game. I worked the boys very hard and put up with no one who put himself before the team. I wanted them to give me 100% on the ice, in games and in practice. I brought a lot of the skills I had gained in my various walks of life to coaching and I believe the boys enjoyed this different approach. I was striving to teach accountability and commitment, as much as hockey skills, and I think they learned a few things along the way.

One of the boys did something dirty which got him kicked out of the game and cost us as a team. I pulled him off the lineup and wouldn't let him play until he apologized to his teammates during practice, which he did. We then set out to follow our plan and had a fantastic year. We won a lot more than we lost and Rob ended up winning the scoring race and MVP for the league.

We qualified for provincials but in doing so Rob broke his hand after getting frustrated during a playoff game and punching a wall after coming off the ice. I could see he was angry when he came off and just as he was throwing the punch I yelled, "Don't do that! You'll break your hand!" He did. We played in regionals without him and won handily (pun intended) and then were off to Cape Breton for Provincials. We saw a doctor for Rob's hand injury, who said that Rob should stay off the ice and not use it at all, because it was a bone that was hard to heal, though not a bad break. As a result, they only put a wrap on it and didn't bother with a full cast.

I asked him what he wanted to do when we left the doctor's office and he said he definitely wanted to play, so we rigged up a kind of splint which gave him some support, but also allowed him to handle his stick with not too much pain. Still, he had very little strength as a result of the break. I think I had to tie his skates, which was a bit of a throw-back to his Atom days.

We made it all the way to the finals and lost the Provincial final by a goal. Rob scored a few during the tournament and had one with one of the hardest shots I've ever seen him take -- with a broken hand yet. Maybe that particular apple didn't fall that far from the tree, after all!

It was a hard loss to take and I felt bad for the boys. I went on to coach the team for three more years after Rob graduated and went on to university. We went to Provincials a couple more times, but only ever managing to bring home a silver medal.

Since I was now speaking in schools a fair bit, a few of my hockey players had me speak in their classes and received credit for it. I never turn down a chance to educate young people, and still do this today when the opportunity presents itself. They ended up with a decent mark a least.

From the moment I started coaching KCA hockey,

there was a gentleman who was always there. He was as much a part of the team as any of the coaches or players and his name was Art Lightfoot. Art was known throughout the league as he covered the league for the local paper and would write a weekly summary of many of the games, complete with pictures that he would take himself during games.

He covered the whole league but did lean towards KCA a bit more because that was his old school. Art would even come to the rink when we practiced, because he just loved hockey. He was one of the founding members of the first hockey school in Canada which, I believe, was held in Kentville in the early fifties. Every kid who played high school hockey knew Art and always spoke to him. I should mention I knew Art a long time before this because he took our wedding photos. Art traveled with us on our team bus trips, and in the four years I coached he only missed a few games.

Every time he saw me, we would talk hockey, even in church. I respected that man more than I can ever put into words because he was a mentor for me and who demonstrated how to be dedicated to the game he so obviously loved.

After Art passed away, I was honoured to build a trophy that is named for him, and presented to this day, and is given at the end of the year for "dedication to the sport". There is also a high school hockey tournament every year named for him as well. I remember him often whenever I walk into that old rink in downtown Kentville.

I loved my job and the people I worked with but the money I was (not) making was stretching us to the breaking point. Eventually a job for Engineering and Maintenance Manager for Annapolis Valley Health was posted, and I thought "why not?" and applied. I had applied for this position a couple of years before and got an interview but didn't get the job. Now there was a new Engineer looking after the entire district, and I knew the site General Manager, after coaching his son the year before, and learned he would be doing the interview along with HR. I did the interview and felt it went well and about an hour or so later I got the call that the job was mine.

It was another seismic shift in careers but, as always, I was more than ready to give it my best and see what I could do with it.

15 MANAGEMENT

I started my new job and my income jumped by about twelve thousand dollars, which both greatly relieved the financial stress on the family and allowed me to stop trying to be a salesman. I was much more suited to a leadership role, for sure.

This position was somewhat uncharted territory for me. I was now responsible for the engineering plants run by around fourteen different Stationary Engineers who supplied everything to the hospitals: heating and cooling, lights, medical air, and many other essentials. I also had a maintenance crew of about sixteen men, looking after six sites from Wolfville to Annapolis Royal and which included the Valley Regional Hospital in Kentville and Soldiers Memorial Hospital in Middleton.

We were part of the Western Regional Health

Authority which also included the South Shore and Yarmouth Districts. We had one Engineer who was in charge of the region, and we would meet collectively on a regular basis. Security also ended up in my lap even though it was contracted out by this time. I was the liaison they worked with when dealing with any issues that came up and which required a decision.

The buildings and equipment weren't a big problem as they were similar to what I was used to on the ships I had been responsible for. The real problem for me was working in a union environment, as a non-union manager, with men who had lost all trust in management. The biggest chore I had in front of me was getting everyone on the same page when we were all reading different books. All of the knowledge I had gained in the navy, and ten years of counselling, would be needed to get this working.

I gave myself two years to turn it around if I could.

Some of the guys knew me from around the hospital but definitely not in an engineering way. They knew me only as an Addiction Counsellor, so in our first meeting I explained my background in the navy and the various trades I was trained in. My first task was to deal with the grievances they felt had not been addressed up to this point. At our second meeting, they gave me their list of about a dozen things that they felt needed to be looked at. I told them to give me a couple of months to look into them and we would get together to go over my findings.

I was able to get answers to the listed items in a shorter time, and met with them to go over everything, and then asked if there were any other issues. They came up with some more things for me to look into. I stated that this would be the final things from the past that I would address, so if they wanted anything else added, it had to be now. Once I had those dealt with, we met again and after reviewing everything and either finding solutions or sound reasons that things were as they were, I explained we could now get to work at what we were all hired to do.

For the most part, I was doing okay with the transition. However, after about two months our Engineer left for another position out of the blue and I was left completely on my own. I had to continue learning my job while at the same time filling in where the Engineer would have handled things. Talk about a steep learning curve!

I ended up going to meetings where I was expected to have answers for leadership to help them make their decisions. I relied on my two counterparts in the other two districts for their knowledge as they had been in their positions for years, and they helped me tremendously during my transition.

I managed satisfactorily over that time period, but it was about six months before another Engineer came on board and made life much better. In a way, I think that time period without a boss helped me, because it enabled me to build confidence in my own decision-making. When you don't have anyone to rely on, you learn to rely on yourself.

One incident illustrates the early relationship I had with my guys: in my office I had put up slogans and positive saying, just like in my hockey dressing rooms, and one day one of the guys was sitting in my office and I noticed he was looking at the slogans. He then said in a disgusted voice, "Are these supposed to motivate us or what?" I looked at him for bit and said, "Hell, no. They are there for my benefit to help remind me to stay positive." I explained to him that I was only responsible for my outlook, and not anyone else's.

I don't really know what he thought of that, but it wasn't any of my business.

I think my favourite parts of the job were getting projects done and coming up with creative ways to get them financed. This suited my solution-focused outlook and fit well in this position. My partner in crime was the Valley Regional's General Manager, Gary, who ended up as my direct boss eventually. There never seemed to be any money to get things done and asking through regular channels fell on deaf ears. Gary and I would dig into any budget available and scrape together enough to get things done using our staff, along with contractors who would go the extra mile, to stretch the money.

I would always hear how it would end up back on my budget, but I always managed somehow to stay close to my budget; if I did go over, I would just explain by pointing to what we had managed to get done. The Department of Health projects required a very close eye because they could get out of hand quickly, but my past experience in overseeing refits helped me in that regard.

I liked the Project Management hat because I got to work with many different contractors and companies. It was always fun picking up on anything that they may have tried to slip through to help their bottom line. My goal was to get the best possible outcome for a fair amount of money. If this happened, it was a win/win and we could do more business down the road.

I always tried to treat the contractors well, as long as they were treating us well.

Two of the first projects I was involved in were bittersweet; one was moving Addiction Services by renovating an unused floor in Soldiers Memorial Hospital, and the other was tearing down the old Sanatorium Miller Building, which was a landmark in Kentville and my first place of employment on leaving the navy. We bought and renovated a building in the industrial park in Kentville and turned it into the Administration headquarters, and both Supply Services and Mental Health services also relocated there. They were very large project, and we got them done pretty much on budget and on time.

One day I got a call from Art Lightfoot, asking if I

would consider coming back and coaching KCA for their last year. The school was closing and KCA and Cornwallis would form a new school called North East Kings Education Centre (NEKEC) the following year. I had finished coaching KCA a couple of years before, when Danny and I coached together for three of the most fun years I ever experienced in coaching. We also received the Coach of the Year award, for one of them. I was more than happy to take this on one more time, and Paul Ross and I co-coached and had a great year. Coincidentally, we lost to Cornwallis in triple overtime to go to Provincials and it was the most intense game I have ever been involved in while coaching.

I went with my remaining players to NEKEC and coached with Roy Brown until all "my kids" graduated two years later. If I remember rightly, we ended up with two more silver medals in Provincials. That was my last time coaching high school hockey, or any hockey, for that matter. I never was able to win a Provincial title while coaching hockey, but the memories and young people I had the privilege to work with will stay with me to the end. All told I coached high school hockey for seven years and it was an amazing experience.

I did, however, coach Jennifer in women's Seven Aside soccer for a few years, until one day I just felt it was over. I told the women that I was doing them a disservice, because my heart was just no longer in it.

That was the official end of my coaching career, which had spanned something over forty years.

I had no idea how much my counselling skills would come into play over the years in dealing with staff problems, mediating between contentious staff, handling upset hospital staff, and many other situations which came up. Dealing with an angry surgeon one moment, a dietitian dealing with failing equipment at mealtime the next, or helping Security handle an upset patient -- any or all tested my abilities, and often in the same day.

What I tried really hard to do was to not react instantly (which is my nature) unless the situation called for it. I would always tell my guys that I would get back to them even, if I had the answer then and there, because one could be continually running around in circles and I wanted to be proactive, not reactive.

One incident was when our air handlers acted up when humidity became very high, and they couldn't handle it. As a result, the hospital had to cancel surgeries. We did the best we could, but the systems weren't designed to handle that level of humidity for an extended period of time.

The head OR doctor called me up and demanded that I guarantee that my equipment wouldn't fail again. I told him I would make that guarantee as soon as he could guarantee me there wouldn't be any further mistakes in the OR. We were all just trying to do what was best for our patients, after all.

Of course, this chapter would not be complete without dealing with the worldwide crisis of Y2K. We had all our guys turned out to help in any way we could for the impending crisis. Most of the hospital was computerized to some degree and the big fear was that the equipment that kept patients breathing and suppling medication would fail, and it would all have to done by hand. We had lots of equipment that was also regulated by computers and had done a lot of preliminary work to ensure we could keep the essential services running -- things like heat, lights, water, air and a host of other things.

The clock counted down and the year 2000 came in with a huge sigh and I must admit to a slight touch of disappointment, because nothing happened. It was the biggest fear- driven disaster hype ever, and people made fortunes off of it. The computer technology department seemed to take off after that. It seemed like every time you turned around there was a new system to learn and I hated it. When they did training and started showing the many different ways to the same thing, I shut down. I would tell them to just show me the best way to do the job and forget the rest. For them it was job security; for me it was just confusing! Remember, I'm a hammer and chisel kind of guy.

The next big event that could have been catastrophic was hurricane-strength nor'easter blizzard of February 2004, White Juan. Fortunately, it was forecasted well-enough ahead of time for us to prepare. Once again everyone was on deck to keep the paths clear and we used the big truck to pick up nurses who couldn't get in. We even had Camp Aldershot (the local army base) on standby if needed.

The entire province was a mess, and it was a tough couple of days just getting cleared out. I stayed at the hospital until the worst was over. We came through it pretty well, all things considered. I had the guys drive me home, but they couldn't get very close, so I busted a trail in waist-deep snow (with some drifts much deeper). Our subdivision banded together with snow blowers to clear our way to where the Main Street was plowed, which I thought was pretty cool, pun intended.

After a couple of years, I finally had my staff all taking personal responsibility for their work. They realized that when something went wrong it wasn't about playing the blame game but about learning a lesson so to avoid the same issue the next time. I managed to visit every site at least once a week so that my guys had a chance to speak face-to-face with me. If I could help them deal with any issues with equipment or people, I was available to do so. Three of the sites had only one lone maintenance guy, and they needed weekly support and someone to talk to who understood where they were coming from.

Maintenance men are not known to be "touchy

feely" types and working in a predominantly female environment was not easy for them. They would be approached to drop what they were doing to help someone, and then have the department they were supposed to be working for angry at them because their project wasn't done. I came up with a solution for all my guys to use. If someone stopped them to ask them to do something, I instructed them to ask that person to contact the department where my guys were supposed to be working and ask if they minded them taking the maintenance guy away to help them. If yes, no problem; if no, ask them to put in a work order and we would get to it.

During this time, I built our house out on the south mountain above Berwick in Rockland. Brian (a good friend) and I had been looking for land that we could possibly buy and divide so we could both build and we weren't having much luck. Judy and I were in Florida on vacation when he called to say he'd bought a piece of land and that the piece next to him was for sale as well. When I came back from vacation, I went to have a look and fell in love with it immediately for the view and what a view it was!

His land was all orchard and the piece I looked at was mostly hayfield and was on a hill with an awesome view of the Annapolis Valley. I walked the land and stood looking out over the valley thinking that this would be the view from my living room. I designed the house around that spot. The land was eight acres more or less, and was being offered for twenty-six thousand, which was for me a great buy.

We had to get the survey done ourselves and, when I did, my surveyor just shook his head and said they had no idea what they were selling because it ended up actually being fifteen acres. I got almost double the land, which made it an amazing deal. We broke ground in September of 2006 and moved into our new place in April 2007, approximately eight months later.

Having all this going on year after year takes its toll, and it did with me.

I was working on some big projects and trying to keep up with all the work, with fewer men, due to cutbacks. The Department of Health had by this time cut about 30 percent of my maintenance staff. I was also trying to talk the Stationary Engineering Assistants (who I had been forced to hire by the Department of Labour) to pick up the slack, with little success. I explained that doing this would add to their job security, but that logic fell on deaf ears.

The last person I ever thought would burn out was me, but it happened. The straw that broke me was something as simple as a misunderstanding. There was someone parked in the wrong parking place and they began making announcements for "Reg Demmy" to please move his vehicle. They continued to make the announcement and it started to drive me nuts. I called my foreman and told him that if "Reg Demmy" didn't move his vehicle soon, to get him towed; I wasn't very nice about it.

The Foreman paused and asked me what I was talking about and I lost it. He finally calmed me down and explained that the announcement was to move a "red Jimmy" and I looked at him and said I was going home.

My mind wouldn't work, and I was having trouble holding a thought. I went to see my doctor and broke down in his office; he put me off work for a month and put me on Celexa, an anti-anxiety medication for six months. I was a mess, very emotional, and had a hard time functioning and just doing everyday things. It took a few weeks before the meds started to help, and I began to come slowly back from the brink. I went back to work after a couple of months but probably shouldn't have.

We were having a meeting and a lady from HR was supposed to come and do a presentation at the start of the meeting. When she didn't show up, we started without her. We were getting into a very heated discussion when she showed up late, and so we stopped to let her do her presentation. I can't recall the subject she was speaking about, but I disagreed with her and was vocal about it. While I was explaining my thoughts on her presentation, I referred to her as "honey" in a dismissive way, I guess, and she left.

A few weeks later I was called to the board room where I was met by two people from Yarmouth HR and was questioned about the incident. Evidently, I was accused of being sexist and insensitive and was instructed that I wasn't allowed to talk to anyone else involved while they investigated the issue. I found out from a few people that she was asking questions of the people who were present during the meeting. I inquired why it was all right for her to talk to people regarding what happened while I wasn't, and I was told flat out that I couldn't.

Long story short, I had to write her a letter of apology (and I did) for my insensitive remark. The head of Valley HR wanted me to apologize in person after that, but I flatly refused. I felt that although I was in the wrong, they had blown it up much bigger than was required, and I didn't appreciate the run-around and the unlevel playing field.

Like I said, coming back early may have resulted in my behaviour, but who knows.

By this time, we had reverted back to District Health Boards once more and a new Management structure was now in place. Gary was now my direct boss, which was a good thing. He was in charge of Support Services, but wasn't an engineer, so after a while they hired an Engineer to look after Support Services, which included us. He came on as a consultant, reviewing all of the department budgets to see what could be done to bring them in line with what the Department of Health would like. He was a Statistical Engineer, and to be honest I don't really know what that is, but he ended up being our boss.

One event caused a shift in me that led to my leaving health care. This event was a flood on level three of Valley Regional Hospital, when a one-inch pipe came apart. It caused a considerable amount of damage before we could get it isolated. The engineer gave me the job to look after the cleanup and repair. I immediately called in the contractors I knew who would respond quickly and they did.

After a couple of days, we had a meeting with the insurance adjustor, and he wanted to bring in the contractors who he was comfortable with. I said I had quotes from my contractors, and they would work together to get it done quickly; he disagreed with everything I had done to that point. I told him I was responsible for all of this and I would stick with what I had in place. There was that stubborn gene again.

The next day our Engineer called me in and told me I wasn't in charge of this project anymore, and the insurance adjuster would have his people look after the remediation and repair. I can only conclude that the insurance adjuster met with him and complained about my ability to handle this situation. My job was thereafter to oversee how it was going. Okay, I thought, so that is what I would do - watch them.

They redid most of what my contractors had already done, wasting time and money, and then started the remediation phase which ended up taking weeks longer and almost doubled the cost. I pointed out several corners cut as well but it didn't seem to matter. I even found them using non-journeymen workers in positions which required a Journeymen-level of expertise. Most, if not all of the contractors, were from outside our area and this bothered me greatly because I literally had spent years building relationships with all the local contractors.

When it was all said and done, the project ended up over time and way over budget. And this was a hospital, not a factory. This was the main hospital in our district and all of its services had been directly impacted. Our Engineer told me later that he should have left the project with me, and I agreed with him. I had written an article a few years before that was called "The Hospital is Our Patient", in which I compared the building and all its systems to a human body. If we didn't look after our patient, the human patients would suffer as a result. The insurance people did not have the same view, obviously.

After that, I decided that as soon as I turned 60, I'd be done; a birthday that was only a few months away. I had told my men that when the job was no longer enjoyable, I'd be gone. Well, it definitely wasn't fun.

Some of the cool and fun things we did over my ten years as the Engineering and Maintenance Manager were breakfasts that Gary, Brian and I would cook for the staff, just for the fun of it, a couple of times a year. We did an outing to a go-cart place in Halifax and had a ball. By this time, we had a really good working relationship which showed in the work accomplished and in the way we all got along, and the trust shown one other.

The best thing we did was put on a golf tournament for all the Support Services in our district. We canvassed all our contractors and the businesses we dealt with for prizes and they came through big time (and were also included in the tournament). There was no winner, and all the prizes were drawn for -- everyone got something. We ran that for seven or eight years, and it went on for a couple of years after I left.

I believe I left the district in better shape than when I started: I helped to introduce new environmental technology in the boiler plant, and two helicopter pads that were fundraised for by the community and built in Kentville and Middleton. Gary and I fought tooth and nail for what we thought would benefit the district, and we won more than we lost.

I promised myself and Judy that I would not let myself get sick again, and when I started to feel myself slipping backwards, I took off the last couple of weeks before I retired. It was not how I wanted to go out but getting sick and being on medication again would not have been the way to go out either, so I did my best to look after myself.

This proved to a good decision because a year after I retired Gary was pushed out, due to restructuring, and more maintenance people were let go as more cutbacks hit. I always found it interesting that cutbacks always affected Support Services primarily. They always said this was so that patients were not affected, but when rooms are dirty, and tests are delayed, and results are slow or supplies aren't getting to the floors, I definitely think that patients are being affected. When infrastructure is affected, everyone is impacted, either directly or indirectly. Again, it's my belief that the hospital was our patient, and at times it was on life support. Smoke and mirrors appear to be alive and well in health care.

Maybe after forty plus years of working non-stop I had finally learned to do just that... stop. I turned sixty on 17 December 2008 and retired in the first week of January 2009.

Of course, my work life wasn't quite finished yet.

16 SECOND CHANCE

After I had been retired for a while, I met up with George who I had worked with in the 28- Day Program, and who was now working in the new Crosbie House -- a private treatment centre in New Minas, Nova Scotia. He suggested that I come in for an interview, so I did.

They had a new manager who I didn't know at all so the interview didn't go as I had expected. I basically laid out what I had for experience and that I would love to work in the field again, but only if it was days and working directly with clients. She said that they weren't looking for anyone at present but would keep my name on file. I was disappointed but I wasn't willing to give up my retirement to start over again.

I figured after that interview I was never going to work in the addictions field again, so I figured I may as well get rid of all my presentations and research and settled into working in my wood shop and on our property.

Judy was still working so I had a lot of time on my own which was great for a while, but I got tired of talking to myself and the dogs. I'm very comfortable with my own company but I'm also the type of person who needs his mind stimulated by other people. I was still reading a lot of books on various subjects but there's just something about face-to-face interaction that gets my brain firing on all cylinders. After a year or so, I volunteered to work on an old bomber for the aviation museum at CFB Greenwood, just to engage with people. I did that for about a year.

Then the phone rang.

I got a call from Reg at Crosbie House saying they were in a pinch. One of the counsellors, John, was out for medical reasons and Reg wondered if I could cover for him for three months or so. I said, "Sure. When do you need me?" He said, "Tomorrow!"

And just like that, I was back.

The next day I was asked if I could do the morning check-in, so I walked into the group and it felt like I had just left on the previous Friday. It was a good feeling, and after I established myself by giving them my background it really felt like I'd never left. I started doing the sessions I was familiar with and then picked up some of John's material but put my own slant on it. I was assigned my first client as their Primary

Counsellor, and I was officially back in the groove.

The three months flew by, and when John returned, I took some time to bring him back up to speed. I figured I'd be back in my shop and working on the old bomber again but to my surprise I was asked to continue working half time, which was originally what I'd wanted to do. I agreed; all I had to do was make sure my schedule was set up so that I was able to make it to all my hockey games.

Retirement, partial or otherwise, does have its advantages!

Shortly after I started, I found out that George was in the hospital and wasn't doing very well. I went to visit him a couple of times and was amazed at his attitude. He was making plans for a trip when he got out. Unfortunately, he passed away a short while later, and I was honoured to build his urn and was asked if it could be built for both him and his wife. It was made from cherrywood and turned out beautifully. I did a really nice inlay of joined hearts from heartwood, which I thought was fitting.

George had been instrumental in resurrecting the 28-Day Program and the second-generation Crosbie House. It was founded on what made the first Crosbie House successful, and carried that format into this version. This was an abstinence-based recovery mode, which had been proven very effective over time, so a big thanks to George and a few others for re-establishing this well-known treatment centre.

I thought it might be interesting to get involved with Family Night, so I started helping on Wednesday evenings. What a learning experience that turned out to be. I had done some family seminars with Evelyn years ago, but only as a guest speaker. Now we were running not only Family Nights, but also the Family Seminars, which allowed me to be exposed to the chaos that we, the addicted, cause in the lives of our loved ones.

My own personal experience of making amends to my family was one thing but having to stand in front of the devastated family members of other addicts and try to explain why we act the way we do was a totally different matter. This was a whole other level of facing emotions, and the goal was to help them see the disease from the addicted point of view. My aim was to help give them a different perspective on something they'd been facing for some time.

Letting them know the difference between when they were dealing with their loved ones and when they were dealing with the disease was now my goal. I asked Judy if she would come and tell her side of our journey during the family seminars, in order to shed some light on that aspect, and it turned out to be very interesting. I would give an overview of my recovery which they listened to, but when Judy told her side of things, they paid extra attention and asked a lot of questions. I was the expert ("ex": being a has-been, and "spurt" being a drip under pressure) while she was, for them, the real deal.

Just as people trying to recover from their addiction want to hear from someone who has done so, those who are trying to survive living with the addict are drawn to people who understand their perspective. Judy was very forthcoming and direct, and it was fun to work with her. I only wish she had been able to do more of the seminars, because she added a lot of reality to the subject matter.

The hardest thing to do was get them to not only focus on what the addict had done (and they all had long lists) but to also look at what part their own behaviour may have played in the dance. Shortly after I started doing this, Lorraine left for another job which meant it was just me for a while. Thank God it didn't last for long. The first family seminar without Lorraine was a baptism by fire, which I did manage to get through, but it was pretty stressful. I was also still doing Program and working with between one and three clients as their Primary Counsellor, so this meant I was very busy. If you've read up to this point, you know that this suits me just fine.

We had a student who did her work placement with us from Success College and when she was done, they hired her on. Molly and I started working together and basically wrote a whole new program for Family Night and the family seminar, as well as for most of the program week on Co-dependence. Co-dependence was her wheelhouse, and my years of experience made us a good team. She was also a whiz with the computer which helped me a lot, because as you know by now, I am more of a "hammer and chisel technology" kind of guy.

We came up with a very sound program for families which added value for the whole program. It got the families involved in their own recovery, which was a tremendous help to them as well as to the addicts. The amazing thing to me was how few family members would take advantage of the opportunity. We made the Family Nights available by Skype so they could take part from the comfort of their own home, but still the numbers were low. This reticence to take part, I think, mirrors the small number of addicts who seek recovery.

The Family Night information followed along with whatever week the program was in. The information of that week was then tailored towards the families and what they were dealing with. The four weeks of the program dealt with addiction, feelings and emotions, family dynamic and relapse. The families usually saw what was covered in those weeks from an entirely different perspective than the clients.

The family seminars always covered different material at a high level, so it could be covered in a day. We started out by going around the room in order to get to know everyone and then asked each what they hoped to get out of the seminar. This was followed by a session with the Program doctor, who explained the medical side of addiction. In the afternoon we showed them a video that talked about how addiction affected five very diverse family units. We ended the day with a Q & A and a course critique. We held the seminars every three months and usually had a full house.

The clients were always nervous that we were talking about them and their progress in the program and were relieved when we assured them that we talked about what the family issues were, and seldom mentioned them at all. Molly and I would, however, often meet with both family members and clients together to help them work through their differences and to establish their "new normal". Without establishing a new normal and moving forward from there, past patterns have a way of re-emerging and derailing the progress made by the addicts and their families.

I remember one meeting with a young man and his mother were checking us out to see if it would be a good place to come for the son, who we'll call John. He was a pretty cool dude who wore his long hair in dreadlocks. He listened to our pitch and asked a few questions but spoke at great length on what he felt he needed. It was obvious that this meeting was more about getting his mother off his back than a genuine search for help. He then said that he felt we were not the place for him and that he would get more help if he went to an ashram in the mountains somewhere. I wished him well.

As they were getting ready to leave, I shook his hand and said, "Someday it would be nice to meet you, John, but I just spent the last hour talking to the addiction." His mother stopped and said, "Oh my God! I see what you mean, and I didn't realize until just now that that is who I've been talking to." This is one of the reasons family members have such a hard time dealing with this disease. They get so wrapped up with their loved ones that they have a hard time separating the person from the problem.

It would have been interesting to be in the car on that drive home.

Another family met with me before their young fellow was ready to leave and felt that when he got home, he would just revert back to his old behaviour. They knew when they confronted him, he would complain that they were treating him like a child, so I suggested that they treat him like an adult and draw up a contract and instruct him on the consequences if he broke it. He would have to accept whatever those consequences were in the contract. That is what adults have to do in the real world, after all. It also made a lot of sense in their situation, given the fact his father was a lawyer.

I don't know if that suggestion was followed but it seemed sensible to me. Families have to hold the addict accountable for their actions or there can be no change, but a crucial aspect is that they must also be aware of the parts they also play, which I know from personal experience.

We had been talking about a course manual for a couple of years and finally decided to do it. We all reviewed our course materials and then started editing and putting it all together. It took us several months to gather and update all the material in order to make sure it reflected all aspects of addiction (and not just to alcohol).

When we were done, we had a manual which we handed out to the clients during their intake and then we followed it. Previously, we would spend a lot of time photocopying for each session which cut down on the time we could spend with clients. Trying to get material ready in this manner was stressful, and the photocopier wasn't always cooperative. This manual allowed us to look for better, more up-to-date, material to stay current with new information.

It was much easier for the clients as they had it all at once and didn't have a bunch of loose paper to juggle. One of the worries was that the clients would get ahead of the course if they had all the material right at the get go. That proved not to be a problem, because most clients only did what they had to do and rarely more, but it sure helped us out a lot.

My favourite thing to do is to create and the fact I had previously trashed all my presentations gave me a chance to re-create them once again as best I could recall. I was able to come up with several new presentations because I'm always exploring new material and information to see if it could be used to help our clients.

Working with Molly to find better ways to get the information across regarding families was a lot of fun, and transformative for me as well. I always enjoy when someone picks my brain because it stimulates me to better ideas and concepts. I think this is why I enjoy group work so much. You're challenged a lot in that format, and this is when I find I come up with new thoughts, because there's no time to over-think things.

I do feel that the time I spent as a manager was very beneficial when it came to working, with clients because it gave me a different perspective, having dealt with so many different walks of life in my past positions. I was also able to put forward different ideas due to the ten years I spent as a manager in health care. My ideas weren't always welcomed, but I felt that by not offering up my experience I was letting things go that could be addressed differently.

I was in a unique position, in that I didn't need the job, so I was able to put a voice to what wasn't necessarily popular. I don't believe I made any earth-shattering changes in that capacity but I'm sure it was good to have someone who didn't worry about their position speak up occasionally on behalf of those who couldn't.

To be honest, I did overstep on a few occasions, which created tension where it really wasn't needed, but I find it hard to watch when people are giving all they have and are not acknowledged for their efforts. I don't believe for a moment that the lack of acknowledgement was intentional, but I do feel it was due to a disconnect. There can sometimes be a lack of knowledge regarding addiction and what is required to work in the field.

Like most other jobs, if you don't understand who you are working for and with, you can be taken advantage of; but nobody, and I mean nobody, can read and manipulate the people around them like an addict. Addicts are able to get what they want at the expense of all else, especially those trying to help them. It is frustrating to work with a group and be called out because someone didn't feel they got a fair deal or disagreed with a topic. The program is set up to deal with difficult issues, and unfortunately a lot of people are yet not ready to deal with those issues and will try to avoid them by causing misdirection.

One of the first things I was asked to do was re-do the Policy and Procedures Manual. This took a considerable amount of time and when completed was delivered to be reviewed by the manager and our Board. This document was to be reviewed yearly and signed off by staff, but to the best of my knowledge it's still sitting on a shelf. I never saw, read, or signed off on it for the next four years.

Bureaucracy is everywhere, I guess, like a snake eating its own tail. I have found that those who work directly with addicts do so because they have a genuine calling to do the work and want the best for the addict. They also understand how hard addiction fights recovery, even when the addicts make the choice to be there. Sugar-coating recovery and making it easy for them is playing directly into their addiction. If someone is forced into treatment, addiction stays in control, for the most part, unless the addict becomes aware of, and accepts, their condition.

I can honestly say that the Program is a fantastic opportunity to work on your recovery and is a huge benefit for those who are ready to make changes and are willing to do the work. I have often said many people recover who don't attend a program at all, but they want recovery because they realize their lives depend on it; something which is illustrated by my own experience.

It amazes me when people come to a program that can greatly enhance their life and put so little effort into it. When clients leave, they are given a written prescription for recovery that they and their counsellor worked out together, and which details what they should do after leaving. This is a program that has been proven to work but many will not follow it, even though they paid a hefty price to get this information.

That is how powerful addiction is, my friends.

Once again, I feel I left my place of employment (Crosbie House) somewhat better than when I started. A three-month term turned into almost five years of doing what I loved, something I never thought I would get to do again.

My work life officially ended after approximately forty-seven years. A work life that started out cutting lines for a surveyor, a stock boy, passing through two different trades in the military, thriving in addiction services by learning and working three positions, a management position with AVRHB and then ending up back helping people again at Crosbie House.

It has been an interesting and fulfilling ride. I did end up going back to Crosbie House and filling in for a couple months while a staff member was off on sick leave, but once that stint ended, I knew I was finally done.

I've heard people say that they are busier in retirement than they were when they were working, and I have definitely found that to be true. My days are always full, and I wouldn't have it any other way. I'm volunteering with two different organizations dealing with those still caught up in the justice system and attend my recovery meetings. Working in my shop and around my property are my places of peace. Our home is the family gathering place, and always has family around. With ten grandchildren, we are seldom alone.

I've had an interesting life to this point, and I am now working on what I've observed and learned along the way in the hopes it may be beneficial to someone who may still be struggling.

This book is the result.
Who knows what may be next?
###

ABOUT THE COVER

Many years ago, there was a painting hung in an AA hall near home. Every time I went to that meeting my eye was drawn to the painting because it spoke to my soul. It was a black and white painting, if memory serves me, which showed a man on his knees inside a bottle with his arms raised and an anguished look on his face. Reaching down from above was a hand and arm with the AA written on the arm.

To me it spoke volumes about the nature of addiction and recovery. The alcoholic was trapped in the bottle and was reaching for the hand of recovery but unable to reach it while still in the bottle. The hand is always there waiting for the alcoholic to crawl out of the bottle so it can help. The hand of recovery is as helpless as the addict in making contact as long as there is active addiction in progress.

I asked around to see if I could find the original painting for the cover of this book, but the hall and painting disappeared long ago. I had done a few paintings over the years so decided to give it a try myself and this is my interpretation of that old painting which had a lasting impact on me. I've added more symbolism to it but that I will leave up to you to determine its meaning.

I hope it may speak to you as it spoke to me many years ago.

ABOUT THE AUTHOR

For the past forty plus years Bob MacDonald has experienced addiction and substance abuse from every angle. First, as a person suffering with addiction himself. Second, as a counsellor & attendant working in a detox program, tending to the needs of people going through early withdrawal, and third, as an addictions counsellor in a certified 28-day treatment facility. Bob has also served as a community health coordinator for families struggling with addiction and as a result has seen first-hand what this issue does to not just the one suffering, but to their family as well.

If you'd like to learn more about the process of addiction
and how to establish good recovery please visit

www.JustRecoveryConsulting.com

Made in the USA
Columbia, SC
31 January 2021